Ohio NOTARY PRIMER

The NNA's Handbook for Ohio Notaries

Ninth Edition

Published by:

National Notary Association
9350 De Soto Avenue
Chatsworth, CA 91311-4926
Telephone: (800) 876-6827
Fax: (818) 700-0920
Website: NationalNotary.org
Email: nna@NationalNotary.org

©2020 National Notary Association
ALL RIGHTS RESERVED. No part of this book may be reproduced in any form without permission in writing from the publisher.

The information in this Primer is correct and current at the time of its publication, although new laws, regulations, and rulings may subsequently affect the validity of certain sections. This information is provided to aid comprehension of state Notary Public requirements and should not be construed as legal advice. Please consult an attorney for inquiries relating to legal matters.

Ninth Edition, Third Printing ©2020
First Edition ©2001

ISBN: 978-1-59767-265-8

Table of Contents

Introduction 1

The Notary Appointment 2

Screening the Signer 8

Reviewing the Document 16

Notarial Acts 23

Recordkeeping 35

Notary Certificate and Stamp 40

Misconduct, Fines and Penalties 47

Electronic and Remote Online Notarization 51

Ohio Laws Pertaining to Notaries Public 63

About the NNA 104

Index 105

Have a Tough Notary Question?

If you were a National Notary Association member, you could get the answer to that difficult question. Join the NNA® and your membership includes access to the NNA® Hotline* and live Notary experts providing the latest Notary information regarding laws, rules and regulations.

Hours
Monday – Friday   5:00 a.m.–7:00 p.m. (PT)
Saturday   5:00 a.m.–5:00 p.m. (PT)

NNA® Hotline Toll-Free Phone Number: 1-888-876-0827

After hours you can leave a message or email our experts at Hotline@NationalNotary.org and they will respond the next business day.

*Access to the NNA® Hotline is for National Notary Association members and NNA® Hotline subscribers only. Call and become a member today.

Introduction

You are to be commended on your interest in Ohio Notary law! Purchasing the *Ohio Notary Primer* identifies you as a conscientious professional who takes your official responsibilities seriously.

In few fields is the expression "more to it than meets the eye" truer than in Notary law. What often appears on the surface to be a simple procedure may, in fact, have important legal considerations.

The purpose of the *Ohio Notary Primer* is to provide you with a resource to help decipher the many intricate laws that affect notarization. In so doing, the *Primer* will acquaint you with all important aspects of Ohio Notary law and with prudent notarial practices in general.

The *Ohio Notary Primer* takes you through the myriad of Notary laws and puts them in easy-to-understand terms, as well as topics not covered by Ohio law but nonetheless of vital concern to you as a Notary.

Whether you're about to be appointed for the first time or are a longtime Notary, we're sure the *Ohio Notary Primer* will provide you with new insight and understanding. Your improved comprehension of Ohio's Notary laws will naturally result in greater competence as a professional Notary Public.

Milton G. Valera
Chairman
National Notary Association

The Notary Appointment

In layperson's language, this chapter discusses and clarifies key parts of the laws of Ohio that regulate Notaries Public. Most of these laws are reprinted in full in "Ohio Laws Pertaining to Notaries Public," beginning on page 63.

In the text that follows, the following abbreviations are used:

ORC. Ohio Revised Code, which contains most of the enacted laws regulating the activities of Notaries Public.

OAR. Ohio Administrative Rule, which is distributed by the Secretary of State's Office.

Additional information about Ohio's requirements for Notaries Public is available on the Secretary of State's website. For step-by-step instructions on the commission application process, applicants also may go to NationalNotary.org/ohio/become-a-notary.

THE NOTARY APPOINTMENT

Application for Appointment

Qualifications. To become a Notary Public in the state of Ohio, the applicant, who is not an attorney in Ohio, must demonstrate to the Secretary of State all of the following: (ORC 147.01)

1. He or she is at least 18 years of age.
2. He or she is a legal resident of the state of Ohio.
3. He or she has completed a background check within the previous six months and with a report showing no convictions or pleading no contest to any disqualifying offenses.
4. He or she has successfully completed an educational program and passed a test.

For attorneys in Ohio, the following requirements must be met:

1. He or she is not a legal resident, but is an attorney admitted to practice law in Ohio, and has a principal place of business or practice in Ohio.
2. He or she is not required to submit a criminal records background check.
3. If he or she is commissioned as a Notary in Ohio prior to the effective date of this amendment, September 20, 2019, they are not required to complete an educational program or pass a test.
4. If he or she applies after the effective date of this amendment, then they must complete an educational program but are not required to pass a test.

Application Submission. The Secretary of State oversees the application process for Notaries in Ohio. The Secretary may also revoke a Notary commission upon presentation of evidence of official misconduct by the Notary. All applications, both new and renewing commissions, must be done electronically (ORC 147.01[C-E]). The application must include:

1. The applicant's name to be used in acting as a traditional Notary Public
2. The applicant's residential address, which must be located in Ohio
3. The applicant's date of birth

4. A criminal records check that is not more than six months old issued by the Bureau of Criminal Identification and Investigation

5. An image of the applicant's signature

6. Evidence of successful completion of three hours of education and testing as required by section 147.021 of the Revised Code

7. An application fee of $15, which must be paid by credit card

Criminal Records Check

To obtain the criminal records check, applicants must apply using the form prescribed and complete the impression sheet prescribed at an authorized agent of the Bureau of Criminal Identification and Investigation. The Secretary of State shall provide a link on its official website to information provided by the Ohio Attorney General's office about the location of the authorized agents of the Bureau of Criminal Identification and Investigation that can complete this function. The criminal records check must not be more than six months old prior to the application being processed (OAR 111:6-3[A][3]).

Education and Exam Requirements

After September 20, 2019, all applicants must complete an educational program prior to being approved by the Secretary of State. Nonattorney applicants must also successfully pass an exam. The education and exam must be completed with a state-approved vendor. A list of approved vendors can be found on the Secretary of State's website. All education and testing must be done within six months of the criminal records check, and a Notary commission must be issued within that same time, or an application must be denied (OAR 111:6-3[A][3]).

For Notaries renewing their commission, they must complete at least one hour of continuing education provided by an approved education vendor (OAR 111:6-2[A]). An exam is not required for renewing Notaries. Attorneys are exempt from completing a continuing education course (OAR 111:6-3[C]).

Renewing a Notary Public Commission

A current Notary Public in Ohio can begin the application process to renew their commission three months prior to the expiration date of their commission. The entire renewal process must be completed prior to a Notary's commission expiration date (ORC 147.031). To renew, the Notary must submit electronically the following:

- A criminal records check that is not more than six months old issued by the Bureau of Criminal Identification and Investigation

- Evidence of successful completion of at least one hour of continuing education provided by the authorized education provider

- An application fee of $15, which must be paid by credit card

If the Notary's commission expires before their commission is renewed, the Notary's commission will not be renewed, and the person must go through the same application process as new Notary applicants (ORC 147.031[D]).

Notary Bond

Not Required. Ohio Notaries are not required to obtain a surety bond.

Liability. As ministerial officials, Notaries generally may be held financially responsible for any and all damages caused by their mistakes or misconduct in performing notarial acts.

If a person is financially injured by a Notary's negligence or failure to properly execute a notarial act — whether performed intentionally or unintentionally — the Notary may be sued in civil court and ordered to pay all resulting damages, including attorneys' fees.

A person need not be named in a document in order to sue a Notary for damages resulting from the Notary's handling of that document. If, for example, a lender accepts a forged, notarized deed as collateral for a loan, the lender might sue to recover losses from the Notary who witnessed the bogus deed.

Errors and Omissions Insurance. Notaries may choose to purchase insurance to cover any unintentional errors or omissions they may make. Notary errors and omissions insurance provides protection for Notaries who are involved in claims or sued for damages resulting from unintentional Notary errors and omissions. In the event of a claim or civil lawsuit, the insurance company will provide and pay for the Notary's legal counsel and absorb any damages levied by a court or agreed to in a settlement, up to the policy coverage limit. Generally, errors and omissions insurance does not cover the Notary for dishonest, fraudulent or criminal acts or omissions, or for willful or intentional disregard of the law.

Commission Recorded by Secretary of State

Recording the Commission. The Secretary of State will maintain a record of the commissions of each Notary appointed and commissioned and will make an index to that record (ORC 147.05[A]).

Jurisdiction

Statewide. Notaries may perform official acts throughout the state of Ohio but not beyond the state borders. A Notary may not witness a signing outside Ohio and then return to the state to perform the notarization; all parts of a notarial act must be performed at the same time and place within the state of Ohio (ORC 147.07).

Term of Office

Five-Year Term. An Ohio Notary Public's term of office is five years, beginning on the effective date shown on the appointment certificate and ending at midnight on the appointment expiration date (ORC 147.03).

Attorney-Notaries. A Notary who is an attorney admitted to practice law in Ohio may hold the office as long as he or she resides in the state or has a principal place of business or primary practice in Ohio, is in good standing before the Ohio Supreme Court, and the commission is not revoked (ORC 147.03).

Notarizing After Commission Expiration. A Notary who knowingly notarizes after his or her commission expires may be fined not more than $500 and become ineligible for reappointment (ORC 147.11). However, an official act performed by a Notary whose commission has expired is considered valid (ORC 147.12).

Change of Address or Name

If Notary Changes His or Her Name. A Notary whose name changes must notify the Secretary of State and appropriate clerk of courts within 30 days of the name change (ORC 147.05).

To report a name change, use the form provided on the Secretary of State's website. Follow the instructions on the form, which must be notarized by another Notary before submitting it to the Secretary. There is a $2 fee for a name change.

If Notary Changes His or Her Address. A Notary whose address changes must notify the Secretary of State using the form provided on the Secretary's website, within 30 days. There is no charge to report an address change to the Secretary of State (ORC 147.05).

Resignation of Appointment

Notification. To resign a commission, use the form from the Secretary of State's website (ORC 147.05). There is no fee to resign a commission. A resignation is appropriate if the Notary moves out of the state. The notice should be sent by certified mail.

The National Notary Association recommends that resigning Notaries destroy or deface their seal of office and any stamp they used to affix information on certificates to prevent their fraudulent use.

Death of Notary

Heirs Notify State. Although not required by Ohio law, the National Notary Association recommends that the Notary's heirs or personal representative inform the office of the Secretary of State of the Notary's death and destroy or deface the deceased Notary's seal of office and any stamp the Notary used to affix information on certificates to prevent their fraudulent use. ■

Screening the Signer

Personal Appearance

Requirement. The principal signer must personally appear before the Notary at the time of the notarization. This means that the Notary and the signer must both be physically present, face to face in the same room, when the notarization takes place. Notarizations may never be performed over the telephone. For personal appearance requirements when performing notarizations remotely online, see the chapter on Electronic and Remote Online Notarization starting on page 51.

Willingness

Confirmation. The Notary should make every effort to confirm that the signer is acting willingly.

To confirm willingness, the Notary need only ask document signers if they are signing of their own free will. If a signer does or says anything that makes the Notary think the signer is being pressured to sign, the Notary should refuse to notarize.

Awareness

Confirmation. The Notary should make every effort to confirm that the signer is generally aware of what is taking place.

To confirm awareness, the Notary simply makes a layperson's judgment about the signer's ability to understand what is happening. A document signer who cannot respond intelligibly in a simple conversation with the Notary should not be considered sufficiently aware to sign at that moment. If the notarization is taking place in a medical environment, the signer's doctor can be consulted for a professional opinion. Otherwise, if the signer's awareness is in doubt, the Notary should refuse to notarize.

Identifying Document Signers

Procedure. When notarizing any signature, Ohio law requires the Notary to positively identify the signer (ORC 147.53[b]).

The following three methods of identification are generally acceptable:

1. The Notary's personal knowledge of the signer's identity (see "Personal Knowledge of Identity," below);

2. The oath or affirmation of a personally known credible identifying witness (see "Credible Identifying Witness," pages 10–11); or

3. Reliable identification documents or ID cards (see "Identification Documents," pages 11–12).

Personal Knowledge of Identity

Definition. The safest and most reliable method of identifying a document signer is for the Notary to depend on his or her own personal knowledge of the signer's identity. Personal knowledge means familiarity with an individual resulting from interactions with that person over a period of time sufficient to eliminate every reasonable doubt that the person has the identity claimed.

Ohio law does not specify how long a Notary must be acquainted with an individual before personal knowledge of identity may be claimed. So, the Notary's common sense must prevail. In general, the longer the Notary is acquainted with a person, and the more interactions the Notary has had with that person, the more likely the individual is indeed personally known.

For instance, the Notary might safely regard a friend since childhood as personally known but would be foolish to consider a person met for the first time the previous day as such. Whenever the Notary has a reasonable doubt about a signer's identity, that individual should be considered not personally known, and the identification should be made through either a credible identifying witness or reliable identification documents.

Credible Identifying Witness

Purpose. When a document signer is not personally known to the Notary and is not able to present reliable ID cards, that signer may be identified by a credible identifying witness. While Ohio statutes do not require an oath or affirmation to be administered to the credible witness, the National Notary Association recommends this additional precaution.

Qualifications. *The Notary Public Code of Professional Responsibility* specifies that a credible identifying witness be personally known to the Notary. In addition, the document signer must be personally known to the credible identifying witness.

Thus, there is a chain of personal knowledge from the Notary to the credible identifying witness to the signer. In a sense, a credible identifying witness is a walking, talking ID card.

Any reliable credible identifying witness should have a reputation for honesty. The witness should be a competent individual who won't be tricked, cajoled, bullied, or otherwise influenced into identifying someone he or she does not really know. And the witness, ideally, should have no personal interest in the transaction requiring a notarial act.

Oath (Affirmation) for Credible Identifying Witness. An oath or affirmation may be administered to the credible identifying witness by the Notary to compel truthfulness.

An acceptable credible-witness oath or affirmation might be:

> Do you solemnly swear that you know this signer truly is the person he/she claims to be, so help you God?
>
> (Do you solemnly affirm that you know this signer truly is the person he/she claims to be?)

Signature in Notary's Journal. If the Notary maintains a journal — although a journal is not required by law, except for recording notarial protests — each credible identifying witness should sign the Notary's journal along with the document signer. The Notary also should print each witness' name and address.

Identification Documents (ID Cards)

Acceptable Identification Documents. Notaries may use reliable identification documents (ID cards) to identify document signers whom they do not personally know. Such cards are considered to be "satisfactory evidence" of identity in lieu of personal knowledge, just as is the sworn word of a personally known credible identifying witness.

The National Notary Association recommends that Notaries rely only on IDs with a photograph, a physical description (e.g., "sex: female, height: 5'5"), and a signature of the bearer. Most government-issued IDs contain all three components.

Examples of acceptable forms of identification include:

1. Ohio driver's license or official nondriver's ID.
2. Driver's license or official nondriver's ID issued by another state.
3. U.S. or foreign passport.

Multiple Identification. While one good identification document or card is sufficient to identify a signer, the Notary may ask for more, especially if the Notary has reasons to suspect that the signer has fraudulent identification.

Unacceptable Identification Documents. Social Security cards, birth certificates, and credit cards can be easily counterfeited and are worthless as primary identifying documents.

Name Variations. The Notary must make sure that the name on the document is the same as the name appearing on the identification presented. In certain circumstances, it may be acceptable for the name on the document to be an abbreviated form of the name on the ID — for example, John D. Smith instead of John David Smith. Last names or surnames, however, should always be the same.

Fraudulent Identification. Identification documents are the least secure of the three methods of identifying a document signer, because phony ID cards are common. The Notary should scrutinize each card for evidence of tampering or counterfeiting, or for evidence that it is a genuine card that has been issued to an impostor.

Some clues that an ID card may have been fraudulently altered with include: mismatched type styles, a photograph raised from the surface, a signature that does not match the signature on the document, unauthorized lamination of the card and smudges, erasures, smears, and discolorations.

Possible tip-offs to a counterfeit ID card include: misspelled words, a brand new-looking card with an old date of issuance, two cards with exactly the same photograph, and inappropriate patterns and textures.

Some possible indications that an identification card may have been issued to an impostor include the birthdate or address on the card being unfamiliar to the bearer or the ID cards seeming brand new.

Signature by Mark

Mark Serves as Signature. A person who cannot sign his or her name because of illiteracy or a physical disability is allowed to make a mark, an "X" for example, as a signature, as long as the mark is witnessed by two persons. Both witnesses also sign the document.

Witnesses for Signature by Mark. For a signature by mark to be notarized, there must be two witnesses to the making of the mark. Although it is permitted for the Notary to also act as one of the witnesses, ideally, the Notary should not act as both. The two witnesses must sign the document. The Notary should write out the marker's name beside the mark.

A mark should also be affixed in the Notary's journal, and the witnesses should also sign the journal.

Notarization Procedures. The marker must be positively identified, just like any other signer. Because a properly witnessed mark is regarded as a signature by custom and law, the Notary is not required to use any other special procedures or certificates.

Although special certificates are not required, the following is a sample acknowledgment form for signature by mark:

State of _____

County of _____

On this the _____ day of _____, 20____ before me, the undersigned Notary Public, personally appeared _____, personally known to be (proven to me on the basis of satisfactory evidence) to be the person who made and acknowledged _____ (his/her) mark on the within instrument in my presence and in the presence of the two persons indicated below who have signed the within instrument as witnesses, one of whom, _____, also wrote the name of the signer by mark near the mark.

Witness my hand and official seal.

(Signature of person taking acknowledgment) (Title or rank)

Commission expiration date

Designated Alternative Signer

An individual whose physical characteristics limit the individual's ability to sign a document presented for notarization may direct a designated alternative signer to sign on the individual's behalf, if all of the following are met (ORC Sec. 147.59[A-B]):

1. The individual clearly indicates, through oral, verbal, physical, electronic, or mechanical means, to the Notary Public the individual's intent for the designated alternative signer to sign the individual's name on the notarial document.

2. Both the individual and the designated alternative signer provide satisfactory identification to the Notary.

3. The designated alternative signer signs the document in the presence of the Notary.

4. The designated alternative signer is not named in the document.

5. The notarial certificate provided to the individual gives the name of the designated alternative signer and states that the document was signed under this section at the direction of the individual.

An individual may use a designated alternative signer to perform an online notarial act if all of the requirements are met.

Notarizing for Minors

Under Age 18. Generally, persons must reach the age of majority before they can handle their own legal affairs and sign documents for themselves. In Ohio, the age of majority is 18. Normally, natural guardians (parents) or court-appointed guardians will sign on a minor's behalf. In certain cases, minors may lawfully sign documents and have their signatures notarized — for example, minors engaged in business transactions or children involved as court witnesses.

Include Age Next to Signature. When notarizing for a minor, the Notary should ask the signer to write his or her age next to the signature to alert any person relying on the document that the signer is a minor. The Notary is not required to verify the minor signer's age.

Identification. The method for identifying a minor is the same as that for an adult. However, determining the identity of a minor can be a problem, because minors often do not possess acceptable identification documents, such as driver's licenses or passports. If the minor does not have acceptable ID, then one of the other methods of identifying signers must be used, either the Notary's personal knowledge of the minor or the oath of a credible identifying witness who can identify the minor. (See "Identifying Document Signers," page 9.)

Foreign-Language Signers. The National Notary Association recommends there should always be direct communication between the Notary and document signer — whether in English or any other language. The Notary should never rely on an intermediary or interpreter to be assured that a signer is willing and aware, given that the third party may have a motive for misrepresenting the circumstances to the Notary and/or the signer.

Refusal of Service

Discrimination. Notaries should honor all lawful and reasonable requests to notarize. A person's race, age, gender, religion, nationality, ethnicity, lifestyle or political viewpoint is never legitimate cause for refusing to perform a notarial act.

A Notary does have the right to refuse a notarization for due cause (e.g., a suspicious ID). According to state officials, Notaries who refuse to provide services should be cautioned of potential discrimination lawsuits for refusing to notarize without reason.

Such reason and any other pertinent information regarding the refusal should be noted in the Notary's journal.

Noncustomers. An employer may limit the services of Notary-employees to business-related notarizations during hours of employment and exclude services to the general public. Notary-employees may refuse to notarize for noncustomers if their employer has limited their services in this manner.

Business Hours. Notaries are not expected to be available to notarize for the public other than during the Notary's normal business hours. However, a Notary may elect to offer notarial services at any hour. ■

Reviewing the Document

Blank or Incomplete Documents

Do Not Notarize. Ohio law prohibits Notaries from notarizing a signature on an incomplete or blank document (ORC 147.141[13]). This is a dangerous practice and a breach of common sense, similar to signing a blank check.

A Notary must never notarize an unsigned, blank or incomplete document. The Notary should insist that all blanks be filled in. Blank spaces not used in a legal instrument should have a line in ink drawn through them so that no one can add to the terms of the instrument after it is signed (HNP).

Blanks in a document should be filled in by the signer prior to notarization. If the blanks are inapplicable and intended to be left unfilled, the signer should line through each space or write "Not Applicable" or "N/A." The Notary may not, however, tell the signer what to write in the blanks. If the signer is unsure how to fill in the blanks, he or she should contact the document's issuer, its eventual recipient or an attorney.

Photocopies & Faxes

Original Signature. A photocopy or fax may be notarized as long as the signature on it is original, meaning that the photocopy or fax must have been signed with pen and ink. Signatures on documents presented for notarization must always be signed with a handwritten, original signature. A photocopied or faxed signature may never be notarized.

Public recorders sometimes will not accept notarized photocopies or faxes, because the text of the document may be too faint to adequately reproduce in microfilming.

Disqualifying Interest

Impartiality. Notaries are appointed by the state to be impartial, disinterested witnesses whose screening duties help ensure the integrity of important legal and commercial transactions. Lack of impartiality by a Notary throws doubt on the integrity and lawfulness of any transaction. A Notary must never notarize his or her own signature, or notarize in a transaction in which the Notary has a financial or beneficial interest.

Financial or Beneficial Interest. Ohio Notaries may not notarize any instrument in which the Notary has an interest. A financial or beneficial interest exists when the Notary is named in the transaction as the grantor, grantee, mortgagor, mortgagee, trustor, trustee, beneficiary, vendor, lessor, or lessee, or as a party in some other capacity (ORC 147.141[C][2]).

Relatives. Although Ohio Notaries are not expressly prohibited from notarizing for a relative, the National Notary Association strongly advises against doing so. Family matters often involve a financial or other beneficial interest that may not be readily apparent at the time of notarization.

Notarizing for family members also may test the Notary's ability to act impartially. For example, a Notary who is asked to notarize a contract signed by his or her brother might attempt to persuade him to sign or not sign. A sibling is entitled to exert influence, but this is entirely improper for a Notary.

Even if a Notary has no interest in the document and does not attempt to influence the signer, notarizing for a relative could subject the document to a legal challenge if other parties to the transaction allege the Notary could not have acted impartially.

Reasonable Care

Responsibility. As public servants, Notaries must act responsibly and exercise reasonable care in the performance of their official duties. If a Notary fails to do so, he or she may be subject to a civil suit to recover financial damages caused by the Notary's error.

Reasonable Care Defined. In general, reasonable care is the degree of concern and attentiveness that a person of normal intelligence and responsibility would exhibit. If a Notary can show a judge or jury that he or she did everything expected of a reasonable person, the judge or jury is obligated by law to find the Notary blameless and not liable for damages.

Complying with all pertinent laws is the first rule of reasonable care for a Notary. And, if there are no statutory guidelines in a given instance, the Notary should go to extremes to use common sense and prudence.

Authentication

Documents Sent Out of State. Documents notarized in Ohio and sent out of state may be required to bear proof that the Notary's signature and seal are genuine and that the Notary had authority to act at the time of notarization. This process of proving the genuineness of an official signature and seal is called authentication or legalization.

These authenticating certificates are known by many different names: certificates of official character, certificates of authority, certificates of capacity, certificates of prothonotary and "flags."

Anyone who requires a certificate of authority should contact the county clerk of the Court of Common Pleas or the Secretary of State's office. It is not the responsibility of the Notary Public to obtain authentication.

The fee for a certificate of authority from a clerk of the Court of Common Pleas varies by county.

Authentication of a Notary's credentials from the Secretary of State requires a fee of $5 and may be obtained by mail by using the

Authentication Request Cover Letter provided on the Secretary of State's website or in person from:

> Ohio Secretary of State
> Client Service Center
> 180 E. Broad Street, Suite 103
> Columbus, OH 43215
> (614) 728-9200

For notarized documents sent from Ohio to other U.S. states and jurisdictions, a single certificate of authority from a clerk of the Court of Common Pleas or from the Ohio Secretary of State is normally sufficient authentication.

Documents Sent Out of Country. If a notarized document will be sent out of the United States, a chain-authentication process may be necessary and certificates of authority may have to be obtained from: the clerk of the Court of Common Pleas, the Ohio Secretary of State, the U.S. Department of State, and different ministries of the involved foreign nation, here and abroad. This chain-certification process can be time-consuming and expensive.

***Apostilles* and the Hague Convention.** Fortunately, more than 100 nations, including the United States, subscribe to a treaty under the auspices of the Hague Conference that simplifies authentication of notarized documents exchanged between any of these nations. The official name of this treaty, adopted by the Conference on October 5, 1961, is *The Hague Convention Abolishing the Requirement of Legalization for Foreign Public Documents*. For a list of the subscribing countries, visit hcch.net/index_en.php.

Under the Hague Convention, only one authenticating certificate, called an *apostille* — meaning "notation" in French — is necessary to ensure acceptance of a Notary signature and seal in subscribing countries.

Immigration

Do Not Give Advice. Nonattorney Notaries may never advise others on the subject of immigration, nor help others prepare immigration documents — and especially not for a fee. Notaries who offer immigration advice to others may be prosecuted for the unauthorized practice of law.

Supporting Documents. Documents not issued by the U.S. Bureau of Citizenship and Immigration Services (USCIS) are often notarized when submitted in support of an immigration or naturalization petition. These might include translator's declarations, bank statements, proof of employment and affidavits of relationship.

Naturalization Certificates. It can be a serious violation of federal law to make a typewritten, handwritten, or any other copy of a certificate of naturalization or notarize it. Severe penalties are prescribed, including imprisonment. (U.S. Penal Code, Section 75 and U.S. Code, Title 18, Section 137.)

Wills

Do Not Offer Advice. Often, people attempt to draw up wills on their own without benefit of legal counsel and then bring these homemade testaments to a Notary to have them "legalized," expecting the Notary to know how to proceed. In advising or assisting such persons, the Notary risks prosecution for the unauthorized practice of law. The Notary's ill-informed advice may do considerable damage to the affairs of the signer and subject the Notary to a civil lawsuit.

Wills are highly sensitive documents, the format of which is dictated by strict and rigid laws. The slightest deviation from these laws can nullify a will. In some cases, holographic (handwritten) wills have actually been voided by notarization because the document was not entirely in the handwriting of the testator.

Do Not Proceed Without Certificate Wording. A Notary should notarize a will only if a Notary certificate is provided or stipulated for each signer, and the signers are not asking questions about how to proceed. Any such questions should properly be answered by an attorney.

Living Wills. Documents that are popularly called living wills may be notarized. These are not actually wills at all, but written statements of the signer's wishes concerning medical treatment in the event that person has an illness or injury and is unable to issue instructions on his or her own behalf.

Durable Power of Attorney for Health Care

Health Care Proxy. A durable power of attorney for health care is another form of advance health care directive. This type of directive differs from a living will in that it appoints a specific person to make decisions on behalf of a principal (the signer) in the event the principal becomes unable to do so due to illness or incapacity.

Signing Requirements. To be legally valid, a durable power of attorney for health care must contain the date of signing and must be signed either by the principal or (if the principal cannot sign in the principal's name) by another adult in the principal's presence and under his or her direction (ORC 1337).

The durable power of attorney for health care is not valid unless it is acknowledged before a Notary Public or is signed by at least two adult witnesses who are present when the principal signs or acknowledges his or her signature. No person who is related to the principal by blood, marriage or adoption may be a witness. The attorney in fact, the attending physician, and the administrator of any nursing home in which the principal receives care are also ineligible to be witnesses.

Unauthorized Practice of Law

Do Not Assist Others with Legal Matters. As a ministerial officer, the nonattorney Notary is generally not permitted to assist other persons in drafting, preparing, selecting, completing, or understanding a document or transaction.

The Notary should not fill in the blanks on a document for other persons, tell others what document they need nor how to draft it, nor advise others about the legal sufficiency of a document — and especially not for a fee.

A Notary, of course, may fill in the blanks on the portion of any document containing the Notary certificate. And a Notary, as a private individual, may prepare legal documents that he or she is personally a party to, but the Notary may not then notarize his or her signature on these same documents.

Notaries who overstep their authority by advising others on legal matters may have their appointments revoked and may be prosecuted for the unauthorized practice of law.

Exceptions. Nonattorney Notaries who are specially trained, certified, or licensed in a particular field (e.g., real estate, insurance, escrow) may advise others about documents in that field, but in no other. In addition, trained paralegals under the supervision of an attorney may advise others about documents in routine legal matters.

Foreign Languages

Foreign-Language Documents. Although Ohio Notaries are not expressly prohibited from notarizing documents written in a language they cannot read, there are difficulties and dangers in doing so: The document may be misrepresented to the Notary, a blatant fraud may go undetected, the Notary may inadvertently perform an incorrect or illegal notarial act, and making a complete journal entry may be difficult.

Ideally, a foreign-language document should be referred to a Notary who reads that language. In many states, the website of the Notary-regulating official has a Notary directory. These directories often include the foreign languages read or spoken by each Notary listed. If a Notary chooses to notarize a document that he or she cannot read, then the Notary certificate should be in English or in a language the Notary can read, and the signature being notarized should be written in characters the Notary is familiar with. ■

Notarial Acts

Authorized Acts

Notaries may perform the following notarial acts (ORC 147.07):

- **Acknowledgments,** certifying that a signer personally appeared before the Notary, was identified by the Notary, and acknowledged freely signing the document. (See pages 25–29.)

- **Oaths and Affirmations,** solemn promises to a Supreme Being (oaths) or solemn promises on one's own personal honor (affirmations) spoken in the Notary's presence. (See pages 29–30.)

- **Depositions,** the written testimony of a witness taken under oath or affirmation (ORC 147.40). (See pages 30–32.)

- **Subpoena Witnesses** in connection with depositions (ORC 5301). (See page 31.)

- **Jurats,** as found in affidavits and other sworn documents, certifying that a signer personally appeared before the Notary, was identified by the Notary, took an oath or affirmation from the Notary, and signed the document in the Notary's presence. (See pages 32–33.)

Other Notarial Officials. In addition to Notaries, the following Ohio officers have the authority to take acknowledgment of certain documents, limited to deeds, mortgages, land contracts, or leases of any interest in real property (ORC 5301.01):

- Judge of a court of record
- Clerk of a court of record
- County auditor
- County engineer
- Mayor

Veteran Affairs Commissioners. Representatives of congressionally chartered veteran organizations may be appointed as Ohio commissioners of veteran affairs, with a three-year term and power to affix a seal in notarizing documents used before the veterans' administration. They may not charge a fee (ORC 147.32).

Unauthorized Acts

Certified Copies. A certified copy is a verified exact duplicate of an original document. A Notary must not "certify that a document is either an original document or a true copy of another record" (ORC 147.141 [A][5])

Requests for certified copies should be directed to the agency that holds or issued the original. For certified copies of birth, death or marriage certificates, and other vital records, the person requesting the copy should be referred to the Bureau of Vital Statistics (or the equivalent) in the state where the event occurred.

This section must not be construed as prohibiting a Notary from notarizing the signature of a holder of a document on a written statement certifying that the document is a true copy of an original document (ORC 147.141 [B])..

Marriages. An Ohio Notary is not authorized to perform marriages.

Acknowledgments

Common Notarial Act. Acknowledgments are one of the most common forms of notarization. Typically, they are executed on documents such as deeds and other instruments affecting real property that will be publicly recorded by a county recorder.

Purpose. In executing an acknowledgment, the Notary certifies three things:

1. The signer *personally appeared* before the Notary at the time of notarization on the date and in the county indicated on the Notary certificate (ORC 147.53).

2. The Notary *positively identified the signer* through either personal knowledge or satisfactory evidence (ORC 147.53 and 147.541) (see "Identifying Document Signers," page 9).

3. The signer acknowledged to the Notary that the *signature was freely made* for the purposes stated in the document and, if the document is signed on behalf of another person, that he or she had proper authority to do so. (If a document is willingly signed in the presence of the Notary, this act can serve just as well as an oral statement of acknowledgment.)

Representative Capacity. A person may sign and acknowledge a document in a representative capacity on behalf of another person or a legal entity (ORC 147.541). Specifically, a representative capacity means:

- For and on behalf of a corporation, partnership, trust, or other entity, as an authorized officer, agent, partner, trustee, or other representative

- As a public officer, personal representative, guardian, or other representative in the specific capacity described in the document

- As an attorney in fact for an absent principal signer

- As an authorized representative of another in any other lawful capacity

A Notary shall not determine the validity of a power of attorney document or any other form designating a representative capacity, such as trustee, authorized officer, agent, personal representative, or guardian, unless that Notary is an attorney licensed to practice law in this state (ORC 147.141 [16]).

Certificates for Acknowledgment. The form of an acknowledgment will be accepted in Ohio under the following circumstances (ORC 147.54):

- The certificate form is prescribed by the laws or regulations of Ohio;

- The certificate is in a form prescribed by the laws or regulations applicable in the place in which the acknowledgment is taken; or

- The certificate form contains the words "acknowledged before me" or their substantial equivalent.

Short Form Acknowledgment Certificates. Ohio law provides acknowledgment certificates for individuals signing on their own behalf, plus a short-form acknowledgment certificate for signers in various representative capacities (ORC 147.55). The authorization of the short forms does not preclude the use of other forms.

- For an acknowledgment in an individual capacity:

    State of _____
    County of _____

    The foregoing instrument was acknowledged before me this _____ (date) by _____ (name of person acknowledging).

    (Signature of Notary, exactly as shown on commission)

    (Notary's printed name)

    (Notarial seal and commission expiration date)

- For a person signing on behalf of a corporation:

    State of _____

    County of _____

    The foregoing instrument was acknowledged before me this _____ (date) by _____ (name of officer or agent title of officer or agent) of _____ (name of corporation acknowledging) a _____ (state or place of incorporation) corporation on behalf of the corporation.

    (Signature of Notary, exactly as shown on commission)

    (Notary's printed name)

    (Notarial seal and commission expiration date)

- For a person signing on behalf of a partnership:

    State of _____

    County of _____

    The foregoing instrument was acknowledged before me this (date) by _____ (name of acknowledging partner or agent), _____ partner (or agent) on behalf of _____ (name of partnership), a partnership.

    (Signature of Notary, exactly as shown on commission)

    (Notary's printed name)

    (Notarial seal and commission expiration date)

- For a person signing as attorney in fact for the principal:

    State of _____

    County of _____

    The foregoing instrument was acknowledged before me this _____ (date) by _____ (name of attorney in fact) as attorney in fact on behalf of _____ (name of principal).

(Signature of Notary, exactly as shown on commission)

(Notary's printed name)

(Notarial seal and commission expiration date)

- For a person signing as public officer, trustee, or personal representative:

    State of _____

    County of _____

    The foregoing instrument was acknowledged before me this _____ (date) by _____ (name and title of position).

    (Signature of Notary, exactly as shown on commission)

    (Notary's printed name)

    (Notarial seal and commission expiration date)

Identification of Acknowledger. In executing an acknowledgment, the Notary must identify the signer through personal knowledge or another form of satisfactory evidence (ORC 147.53 and 146.541). (See "Identifying Document Signers," page 9.)

Signing in Notary's Presence Not Required. For an acknowledgment, the document does not have to be signed in the Notary's presence. Rather, the document signer need only acknowledge having made the signature. As long as the signer appears before the Notary at the time of notarization to acknowledge having signed, the Notary may execute the acknowledgment.

The document could have been signed an hour before, a week before, a year before, etc. — as long as the signer appears before the Notary with the signed document at the time of notarization to admit that the signature is his or her own. (Note: for a jurat notarization, the document must be signed in the Notary's presence. See "Jurats," pages 32–33.)

Additional Witnesses Required for Certain Documents. Certain documents must be acknowledged to be valid and recorded. For example, deeds, mortgages, land installment contracts and leases for a term exceeding three years are required to be acknowledged. Prior to 2002, certain documents, in addition to being notarized, were required to be signed in the presence of at least two witnesses, one of whom could be the Notary. However, that requirement has been eliminated in most instances.

Terminology. In discussing the notarial act of acknowledgment, it is important to use the proper terminology. A Notary takes or executes an acknowledgment, while a document signer makes or gives an acknowledgment.

Oaths and Affirmations

Purpose. An oath is a solemn, spoken pledge to a Supreme Being. An affirmation is a solemn, spoken pledge on one's own personal honor, with no reference to a Supreme Being. Both are usually a promise or pledge of truthfulness or fidelity and have the same legal effect.

In taking an oath or affirmation in an official proceeding, a person may be subject to criminal penalties for perjury should he or she fail to be truthful.

An oath or affirmation can be a full-fledged notarial act in its own right, as when giving an oath of office to a public official, or it can be part of the process of notarizing a document (e.g., executing a jurat or swearing in a credible identifying witness).

A person who morally objects to taking an oath — pledging to a Supreme Being — may instead be given an affirmation, which does not refer to a Supreme Being.

Power to Administer. Ohio Notaries may administer any oath or affirmation required by state law, including oaths of office to public officials (ORC 147.07).

Wording for Oath or Affirmation. If law does not dictate otherwise, an Ohio Notary may use the following or similar words in administering an oath or affirmation:

- Oath (Affirmation) for an affiant signing an affidavit or a deponent signing a deposition:

Do you solemnly swear that the statements made in this affidavit (or deposition) are the truth, the whole truth and nothing but the truth, so help you God?

(Do you solemnly affirm that the statements made in this affidavit (or deposition) are the truth, the whole truth and nothing but the truth?)

- Oath (Affirmation) for a credible identifying witness identifying a document signer who is in the Notary's presence:

Do you solemnly swear that you know this signer truly is the person he/she claims to be, so help you God?

(Do you solemnly affirm that you know this signer truly is the person he/she claims to be?)

The oath or affirmation wording must be spoken aloud, and the person taking the oath or affirmation must answer affirmatively with, "I do," "Yes," or the like. A nod or grunt is not a clear and sufficient response. If a person is mute and unable to speak, the Notary may rely on written notes to communicate.

Ceremony and Gestures. To impress upon the oath- or affirmation-taker the importance of truthfulness, the Notary is encouraged to lend a sense of ceremony and formality to the oath or affirmation. During administration of an oath or affirmation, the Notary and person taking the oath or affirmation traditionally raise their right hands, though this is not a legal requirement. Notaries generally have discretion to use the words and gestures that they feel will most compellingly appeal to the conscience of the oath-taker or affirmant.

Depositions and Affidavits

Purpose. A deposition is a signed transcript of the signer's oral statements taken down for use in a judicial proceeding. This deposition signer is called a deponent. An affidavit is a signed statement made under oath or affirmation by a person called an affiant, and it is used for a variety of purposes, both in and out of court. For both a deposition and an affidavit, the Notary must administer an oath or affirmation and complete some form of jurat, which the Notary signs and seals.

Depositions. With a deposition, both sides in a lawsuit or court case have the opportunity to examine and cross-examine the deponent. Questions and answers are transcribed into a written statement. Used only in judicial proceedings, a deposition is then signed and sworn to before an oath-administering official such as a Notary Public.

Although Ohio law authorizes every Notary Public to take and certify depositions, usually only court stenographers are called upon to do so. It is recommended that if a Notary is requested to take a deposition, he or she should consult an attorney before deciding to exercise this power.

Subpoena of Witnesses. If requested, a Notary Public may subpoena the witnesses to be examined in a deposition (ORC 147.07). The subpoena is to be served by the sheriff and any constable of the county, or by a person designated by the Notary. A person serving the notice other than a sheriff, coroner, or constable must make an affidavit that he or she served the party. The notice must be served on the adverse party or his or her attorney, or left at the residence of the party or the party's agent. The notice must be served to allow the subpoenaed party time, exclusive of Sundays, the day of service and one day for preparation to arrive at the specified place in the notice.

The statute gives Notaries the power not just to serve the notice, but also to compel witnesses to be present and to punish witnesses for not complying with the subpoena, but a discussion of these duties is outside of the scope of this Primer. A Notary who is requested to serve a witness, compel a witness to attend or punish witnesses for non-attendance should consult an attorney for further instructions.

Affidavits. Affidavits are used in and out of court for a variety of purposes, from declaring losses to an insurance company to declaring U.S. citizenship before traveling to a foreign country. An affidavit is a document containing a statement voluntarily signed and sworn to or affirmed before a Notary or other official with oath-administering powers. If used in a judicial proceeding, only one side in the case need participate in the affidavit process, in contrast to the deposition.

Certificate for Depositions and Affidavits. Depositions and affidavits require jurat certificates. (See "Jurats," pages 32–33.)

Oath (Affirmation) for Depositions and Affidavits. If no other wording is prescribed in a given instance, a Notary may use the following language in administering an oath (affirmation) for an affidavit or deposition:

> Do you solemnly swear that the statements made in this affidavit (or deposition) are the truth, the whole truth and nothing but the truth, so help you God?
>
> (Do you solemnly affirm that the statements made in this affidavit [or deposition] are the truth, the whole truth and nothing but the truth?)

Jurats

Part of Verification. In notarizing affidavits, depositions, and other forms of written verification requiring an oath by the signer, the Notary normally executes a jurat.

Purpose. While the purpose of an acknowledgment is to positively identify a document signer, the purpose of a verification with jurat is to compel truthfulness by appealing to the signer's conscience and fear of criminal penalties for perjury.

In executing a jurat, a Notary certifies that:

1. The signer *personally appeared* before the Notary at the time of notarization on the date and in the county indicated on the Notary certificate.

2. The Notary personally knows the signer or was *positively identified* through satisfactory evidence (see "Identifying Document Signers," pages 9–12).

3. The Notary witnessed the *signer sign the document* at the time of notarization.

4. The Notary administered an oath or affirmation to the signer.

Certificate for a Jurat. A jurat is the wording, "Subscribed and sworn to (or affirmed) before me on this _____ (date) by

_____ (name of signer) ..." or similar language. The following jurat language meets the requirements:

> State of Ohio
>
> County of _____
>
> Sworn to (or affirmed) before me and signed in my presence this day of _____, 20____.
>
> (Signature of Notary, exactly as shown on commission)
>
> (Notary's printed name)
>
> (Notarial seal and commission expiration date)

Identification of Signer. In executing a jurat, the Notary must identify the signer either through identification documents or a credible identifying witness. (See "Identifying Document Signers," page 9.)

Wording for Jurat Oath (Affirmation). If not otherwise prescribed by law, an Ohio Notary may use the following or similar to administer an oath (or affirmation) in conjunction with a jurat:

> Do you solemnly swear that the statements made in this document are the truth, the whole truth and nothing but the truth, so help you God?
>
> (Do you solemnly affirm that the statements in this document are the truth, the whole truth and nothing but the truth?)

Oath or Affirmation Not Administered. Failing to administer any oath or affirmation as required by law could subject the Notary to a fine and revocation of the Notary's commission (ORC 147.14).

Fees for Notarial Services

Maximum Fees. The following maximum fees for performing notarial acts are allowed by Ohio law (ORC 147.08):

- **Acknowledgments — $5** per document. For taking an acknowledgment, the Notary may charge no more than $5 for each document notarized.

- **Oaths and Affirmations Without Signature — $5.** For administering an oath or affirmation without requiring the person taking the oath or affirmation to sign a document, the Notary may charge no more than $5 for each person taking the oath or affirmation.
- **Jurats — $5.** For taking and certifying an affidavit. (This fee covers administration of the oath or affirmation.)
- **Depositions (customary fee).** For taking a deposition, the Notary may charge whatever fees are customary (ORC 2319.27).

Travel Fees. Charges for travel by a Notary are not specified by law. Such fees are proper only if Notary and signer agree beforehand on the amount to be charged. The signer must understand that a travel fee is not stipulated in law and is separate from the notarial fees described above (ORC 141.08 [D]).

Overcharging. Charging more than the legally prescribed fees may result in the loss of the Notary's commission with no possibility for reinstatement (ORC 147.13). ∎

Recordkeeping

Journal of Notarial Acts

Recommended. Ohio statute requires Notaries to have an official register for the recording of protests (ORC 147.04), and the *Handbook and Notarial Journal for Notaries Public* states, "it is not necessary to obtain a registry unless, and until a Notary is called upon to make a notarial protest." Nevertheless, the *Handbook* also prints sample journal pages with spaces for the date, name of person(s), fee paid, type of notarization, ID used and comments for each notarial act.

The National Notary Association and other Notary-regulating officials across the nation recommend for every Notary to keep a detailed, accurate and sequential journal of all notarial acts.

Prudent Notaries keep detailed and accurate journals of their notarial acts for many reasons:

- Keeping records is a businesslike practice that every conscientious businessperson and public official should engage in. Not keeping records of important transactions, whether private or public, is risky.

- A Notary's recordbook protects the public's rights to valuable property and to due process by providing documentary evidence in the event a document is lost or altered, or if a transaction is later challenged.

- In the event of a civil lawsuit alleging that the Notary's negligence or misconduct caused the plaintiff serious financial harm, a detailed journal of notarial acts can protect the Notary by showing that reasonable care was used to identify a signer. It would be difficult to contend that the Notary did not bother to identify a signer if the Notary's journal contains a detailed description of the ID cards that the signer presented.

- Since civil lawsuits arising from a contested notarial act typically take place three to six years after the act occurs, the Notary normally cannot accurately testify in court about the particulars of a notarization without a journal to aid the Notary's memory.

- Journals of notarial acts prevent baseless lawsuits by showing that a Notary did use reasonable care, or that a transaction did occur as recorded. Journal thumbprints and signatures are especially effective in defeating such groundless suits.

Journal Entries. The Notary's journal should contain the following information for each notarial act performed:

1. The date, time of day and type of notarization (e.g., jurat, acknowledgment, etc.).

2. The type (or title) of document notarized (e.g., deed of trust, affidavit of loss, etc.), including the number of pages and the date of the document.

3. The signature, address, and printed name of each document signer and witness.

4. A statement as to how the signer's identity was confirmed (if by personal knowledge, the journal entry should read "Personal Knowledge"; if by satisfactory evidence, the journal entry must contain either: a description of the ID card accepted, including the type of ID, the government agency issuing the ID, the serial or identifying number and the date of issuance or expiration; or, the signature of any credible identifying witness — see "Credible Identifying Witness," pages 10–11).

5. Any other pertinent information, including the fee charged for the notarial service.

Document Dates. If the document has a specific date on it, the Notary should record that date in the journal of notarial acts. Often the only date on a document is the date of the signature that is being notarized. If the signature is undated, however, the document may have no date on it at all. In that case, the Notary should record "no date" or "undated" in the journal.

For acknowledgments, the date the document was signed must either precede or be the same as the date of the notarization; it may not follow it. For a jurat, the date the document was signed and the date of the notarization must be the same.

A document whose signature is dated after the date on its Notary certificate risks rejection by a recorder, who may question how the document could have been notarized before it was signed.

Method of Identification. Although recording the method used to identify each signer is not required by law, it is prudent to do so. If the signer is personally known, the Notary should indicate that in the journal. If the signer is identified using an ID document, the Notary should record the document's issuer, type, serial number, and date of issuance or expiration. If the signer is identified by a credible identifying witness, the Notary should record the witness's printed name and address and have the witness sign the journal.

Journal Signature. Perhaps the most important entry to obtain is the signer's signature. A journal signature protects the Notary against claims that a signer did not appear and is a deterrent to forgery, because it provides evidence of the signer's identity and appearance before the Notary.

To check for possible forgery, the Notary should compare the signature that the person leaves in the journal of notarial acts with the signatures on the document and on the IDs. The signatures should be at least reasonably similar.

The Notary also should observe the signing of the journal. If the signer appears to be laboring over the journal signature, this may be an indication of forgery in progress.

Since a journal signature is not required by law, the Notary may not refuse to notarize if the signer declines to leave one.

Journal Thumbprint. Many Notaries are asking document signers to leave a thumbprint in the journal. The journal thumbprint protects the Notary against claims that a signer did not appear and is a strong deterrent to forgery, because it represents absolute proof of the signer's identity and appearance before the Notary.

Provided the signer is willing, nothing prevents a Notary from asking for a thumbprint for every notarial act. Since a thumbprint is not required by law, however, the Notary may not refuse to notarize if the signer declines to leave one.

Additional Entries. Notaries may include additional information in the journal that is pertinent to a given notarization. Many Notaries, for example, enter the telephone number of all signers and witnesses, as well as the address where the notarization was performed, if not at the Notary's office. A description of the document signer's demeanor (e.g., "The signer appeared very nervous") or notations about the identity of other persons who were present for the notarization may also be pertinent.

One important entry to include is the signer's representative capacity — whether the signer is acting as attorney in fact, trustee, guardian, corporate officer, or in another capacity — if not signing on his or her own behalf.

Complete Entry Before Certificate. The prudent Notary completes the journal entry before filling out the Notary certificate on a document. This prevents the signer from suddenly leaving with the notarized document before vital information can be entered in the journal.

Journal Inspection and Copies. A Notary's journal contains valuable information of documentary transactions. In certain instances, a transacting or relying party or any member of the public affected by the document may request to inspect the Notary's journal or may ask the Notary to provide a photocopy of a particular entry. The National Notary Association discourages "fishing expeditions" through the Notary's journal by persons without some minimal knowledge of the transaction.

Accordingly, the National Notary Association recommends that in order to inspect the journal or to receive a photocopy of a journal entry, the inquiring person should present a written request specifying at least the month and year of the notarization at issue, as well as the type of document and names of signers. Upon providing this minimum information, the Notary may allow the person to inspect the line item of the notarization in question, but no other, or the Notary may provide a photocopy of the line item.

Never Surrender Journal. Notaries should never surrender control of their journals to anyone, unless expressly subpoenaed by a court order. Even when an employer has paid for the Notary's official journal and seal, they go with the Notary upon termination of employment; no person but the Notary may possess and use this official tool of the Notary's office. ■

Notary Certificate and Stamp

Notary Certificate

Requirement. In notarizing any document, a Notary must complete a Notary certificate. The certificate is wording that indicates exactly what the Notary has certified. The Notary certificate wording may appear on the document itself or on an attachment to it. The certificate should contain (ORC 147.54[G]):

1. A *venue* indicating where the notarization is being performed. "State of Ohio, County of _____," is the typical venue wording, with the county name inserted in the blank. The letters "SS." or "SCT." sometimes appear after the venue; they abbreviate the traditional Latin word scilicet, meaning "in particular" or "namely."

2. A *statement of particulars* that indicates what the notarization has attested. An acknowledgment certificate would include such wording as: "This instrument was acknowledged before me on _____ (date) by _____ (name of signer)." A jurat certificate would include such wording as: "Signed and sworn to (or affirmed) before me on _____ (date) by _____ (name of signer)."

3. A *testimonium clause,* which may be optional if the date is included in the statement of particulars: "Witness my hand

and official seal, this _____ day of _____." Sometimes, the date is omitted from the testimonium clause. In this phrase, the Notary formally attests to the truthfulness of the preceding facts in the certificate. "Hand" means signature.

4. The *official signature of the Notary,* exactly as the name appears on the Notary's commissioning paper. The notary's printed name, displayed below the notary's signature or inked stamp. A notary with a physical disability that limits the notary's ability to sign a certificate may use a signature stamp after submitting an example of the stamp to the Secretary of State.

5. The *official seal of the Notary,* placed near but not over the Notary's signature.

Completing the Certificate. When filling in the blanks in the Notary certificate, Notaries should either type or print neatly in dark ink.

Correcting a Certificate. When filling out the certificate, the Notary needs to make sure any preprinted information is accurate. For example, the venue — the state and county in which the notarial act is taking place — may have been filled in prior to the notarization. If the preprinted venue is incorrect, the Notary must line through the incorrect state and/or county, write in the proper site of the notarization, and initial and date the change.

A Notary must not alter anything in a written instrument after it has been signed by anyone. Also, a Notary must not amend or alter a notarial certificate after the notarization is complete. (ORC 147.141 [A] [11-12])

Certificate Forms. When certificate wording is not preprinted on the document, or when preprinted wording is not acceptable, the Notary may attach a certificate form. This form typically is stapled to the document's left margin following the signature page.

If the certificate form is replacing unacceptable preprinted wording, the Notary should line through the preprinted wording and write below it, "See attached certificate." If the document has no preprinted wording, however, the Notary should not add this notation. Those words could be viewed as an unauthorized change to the document.

To prevent a certificate form from being removed and fraudulently placed on another document, the Notary may add a brief description of the document to the certificate: "This certificate is attached to a _____ (title or type of document), dated _____ (date), of _____ (number) pages, signed by _____ (name[s] of signer[s]."

The National Notary Association offers certificate forms that have similar wording preprinted on them; otherwise, the Notary will have to print, type, or stamp this information on each certificate form used.

Finally, when Notaries attach a certificate form to a document, they always should note in their journals that they did so, as well as the means by which they attached the certificate to the document: "Certificate form stapled to document, following signature page."

While fraud-deterrent steps such as these can make it much more difficult for a certificate form to be removed and misused, there is no absolute protection against its removal and misuse. While a certificate form remains in their control, however, Notaries must absolutely ensure that it is attached only to its intended document.

Document Recording Requirements. House Bill 525 established the following standards for documents presented for recording (ORC 317.114[A]):

- Minimum paper size is 8½ x 11 inches
- Maximum paper size is 8½ x 14 inches
- Side margins of one inch
- Bottom margin of 1½ inches
- First page top margin of three inches to accommodate the recorder's certification or indorsement stamp
- A 1½-inch top margin on each page in addition to the first
- Print size not smaller than 10-points
- Use of blue or black ink color only

Notaries must ensure that their seal images do not protrude into the assigned margins of the documents. An impression of the Notary's official seal that protrudes into the margins could be grounds for the recorder to charge an additional fee to record the document.

Notaries should use only blue or black ink to affix a signature and seal impression and, if possible, use an official inking seal with information in at least 10-point type.

Highlighting Disallowed. In addition, the new recording standards do not permit documents presented for recording to contain highlighting of any kind (ORC 317.114[A][5]). Lenders and closing agents might add highlighting to loan documents to ensure that a Notary Signing Agent does not "miss" a signature or initial. Under the new law, these documents would be subject to a penalty fee.

Exemptions. The law exempts the following documents from the new recording format requirements (ORC 317.114[B]):

- Any document that originates with any court or taxing authority

- Any document authorized to be recorded under section 317.24 of the Revised Code

- Any plat, as defined in section 711.001 of the Revised Code

- Any document authorized to be recorded that originates from any state or federal agency

- Any document executed before the effective date of the new law

Do Not Pre-Sign or Pre-Seal Certificates. A Notary must never sign and/or seal certificates ahead of time or permit other persons to attach a Notary certificate form to a document. A Notary must never give or mail an unattached, signed and sealed certificate form to another person and trust that person to attach it to a particular document, even if asked to do so by a signer who previously appeared before the Notary.

These actions could facilitate fraud or forgery, and, since such actions would be indefensible in a civil court of law, they could subject the Notary to lawsuits to recover damages resulting from the Notary's neglect or misconduct.

Selecting Certificates. Nonattorney Notaries should never select Notary certificates for any transaction. It is not the role of a nonattorney Notary to decide what type of certificate — and thus what type of notarization — a document needs. As ministerial officials, Notaries generally follow instructions and fill out forms that have been provided for them; they do not issue instructions and decide which forms are appropriate in a given case.

A Notary Public may explain to a signer the difference between an acknowledgment and a jurat, but must not, unless that Notary is an attorney, advise the person on the type of notarial act that best suits a situation. (ORC 147.542 [H]).

If a document is presented to a Notary without certificate wording and if the signer doesn't know what type of notarization is appropriate, the signer should be asked to find out what kind of notarization and certificate are needed. Usually, the agency that issued the document or the one that will be accepting the document can provide this information. Selecting certificates may be considered the unauthorized practice of law.

Notary Seal

Requirement. Ohio Notaries are required to possess an official seal of office, and its use is customary on every document notarized. Statutes state that an instrument notarized without a seal being affixed is still valid, provided all other requirements have been met (HNP and ORC 147.04).

There is a very practical reason for using a Notary seal on notarized documents sent to other states and nations: the absence of a seal may delay, or, on occasion in foreign nations, prevent the document's acceptance.

In addition, many Notaries elect to use an inking or embossing seal to impart an appropriate sense of ceremony to their official acts.

Embossing and Inking Seals. There are two types of Notary seals, both of which are acceptable for use in Ohio: the traditional metal embosser, which crimps its impression onto a paper surface and aids in distinguishing photocopies from originals; and the more modern inking stamp, usually with a rubber face, which imprints a photocopiable impression on the paper. (Many Ohio Notaries also use an inking stamp to affix their name, commission expiration date, and other required information. (See "Required Information," below.) (ORC 147.04).

Format and Required Information. The Ohio Notary seal is circular or rectangular, consisting of the state's coat of arms within a 3/4" to one-inch circle, and surrounded by the words "Notary Public," "Notarial Seal," or words to that effect, the name of the Notary, and the words "State of Ohio."

The Notary has the option of omitting his or her name from the official seal and instead typing, printing, or stamping it near the Notary's signature on each document (ORC 147.04).

Placement of the Seal Impression. The Notary's official seal impression should be placed near the Notary's signature on the Notary certificate, but it should not overlap the signature or any wording. Some recorders will reject documents if writing or document text intrudes within the borders of the Notary's seal.

If there is no room for a seal, the Notary may have no choice but to complete and attach a certificate form that duplicates the Notary wording on the document.

L.S. The letters "L.S." — abbreviating the Latin term *locus sigilli*, meaning "place of the seal" — appear on many Notary certificates to indicate where the Notary seal should be placed. While an embossing seal may be affixed over these letters, an inking stamp should be imprinted near, but not over, the letters.

Illegible Seal. If an initial seal impression is unreadable and there is ample room on the document, another impression can be affixed nearby. The illegibility of the first impression will indicate why a second seal impression was necessary. The Notary should then record in the journal that a second impression was applied.

A Notary should never attempt to fix an imperfect seal impression with pen, ink or correction fluid. This may be viewed as evidence of tampering and cause the document to be rejected by a receiving agency.

Personal Property. The seal — along with the journal and the Notary's certificate of appointment — is considered the personal property of the Notary, regardless of who paid for the seal, journal, or commission. ■

Misconduct, Fines and Penalties

Prohibited Acts

Notaries in Ohio are forbidden to do any of the following (ORC 147.141[A-C]):

1. Perform a notarial act with regard to a record or document executed by the Notary;

2. Notarize the Notary's own signature;

3. Take the Notary's own deposition;

4. Perform a notarial act if the Notary has a conflict of interest with regard to the transaction in question;

5. Certify that a document is either of the following:

    a. An original document;

    b. A true copy of another record.

6. Use a name or initial in signing certificates other than that by which the Notary Public is commissioned;

7. Sign notarial certificates using a facsimile signature stamp unless the Notary Public has a physical disability that limits

or prohibits the Notary's ability to make a written signature and unless the Notary has first submitted written notice to the Secretary of State with an example of the facsimile signature stamp;

8. Affix the Notary's signature to a blank form of an affidavit or certificate of acknowledgment and deliver that form to another person with the intent that it be used as an affidavit or acknowledgment;

9. Take the acknowledgment of, or administer an oath or affirmation to, a person who the Notary Public knows to have been adjudicated mentally incompetent by a court of competent jurisdiction, if the acknowledgment or oath or affirmation necessitates the exercise of a right that has been removed;

10. Notarize a signature on a document if it appears that the person is mentally incapable of understanding the nature and effect of the document at the time of notarization;

11. Alter anything in a written instrument after it has been signed by anyone;

12. Amend or alter a notarial certificate after the notarization is complete;

13. Notarize a signature on a document if the document is incomplete or blank;

14. Notarize a signature on a document if it appears that the signer may be unduly influenced or coerced so as to be restricted from or compromised in exercising the person's own free will when signing the document;

15. Take an acknowledgment of execution in lieu of an oath or affirmation if an oath or affirmation is required;

16. Determine the validity of a power of attorney document or any other form designating a representative capacity, such as trustee, authorized officer, agent, personal representative, or guardian, unless that Notary is an attorney licensed to practice law in this state.

Division (A)(5) of this section shall not be construed as prohibiting a Notary from notarizing the signature of a holder of a document on a written statement certifying that the document is a true copy of an original document.

"Conflict of interest" means either of the following:

1. The Notary has a direct financial or other interest in the transaction in question, excluding the fees authorized under this chapter.

2. The Notary is named, individually or as a grantor, grantee, mortgagor, mortgagee, trustor, trustee, beneficiary, vendor, lessor, or lessee, or as a party in some other capacity to the transaction.

A nonattorney Notary is not allowed to represent or advertise themselves as an immigration consultant or an expert in immigration matters (ORC 147.142[A]).

A nonattorney Notary must not do any of the following in regards to the unauthorized practice of law (ORC Sec.147.142[B]):

1. Provide any service that constitutes the unauthorized practice of law in violation of section 4705.07 of the Revised Code;

2. State or imply that the Notary is an attorney licensed to practice law in this state;

3. Solicit or accept compensation to prepare documents for or otherwise represent the interest of another person in a judicial or administrative proceeding, including a proceeding relating to immigration to the United States, United States citizenship, or related matters;

4. Solicit or accept compensation to obtain relief of any kind on behalf of another from any officer, agency, or employee of this state or of the United States;

5. Use the phrase *"notario"* or *"notario publico"* to advertise the services of a Notary Public, whether by sign, pamphlet, stationery, or other written communication, or by radio, television, or other non-written communication.

Overcharging. A Notary who charges more than the maximum fees permitted by law is subject to removal from office and will be ineligible for reappointment (ORC 147.13).

Civil Lawsuit

Liability. As a ministerial official, an Ohio Notary is liable for all damages caused by any intentional or unintentional misconduct or neglect. A civil lawsuit against the Notary may seek financial recovery against all of the Notary's personal assets. ■

Electronic and Remote Online Notarization

Electronic Notarization Rules

Any Notary Public may obtain an electronic seal and signature for the purposes of notarizing documents (ORC 147.591[C]). There is not a separate registration to notarize electronic documents. However, the Notary will need to purchase an electronic seal and electronic signature prior to notarizing electronic documents. The procedures for notarizing an electronic document are similar to traditional paper notarizations (personal appearance is required, identifying the signer is a must, etc.). The differences will be that the Notary is notarizing an electronic document on a computer rather than a paper document, and the Notary certificate will need to reflect that it was notarized electronically.

An electronic document that is signed in the physical presence of the Notary Public with an electronic signature and notarized with an electronic seal must be considered an original document (ORC Sec.147.591[B][1]).

A printed copy of a document that was signed electronically and was properly notarized by a Notary must be accepted by county auditors, engineers, and recorders to the same extent as other electronic recording methods as long as a proper notarial certificate is included (ORC Sec. 147.591[B][2]).

Electronic Notary Certificate Forms

For electronic notarial acts performed by a Notary for a principal in the Notary's physical presence, the Notary certificate forms provided in section 147.55 of the Revised Code may be used if the forms include this statement or something similar: "This certificate pertains to an electronic notarial act performed with the principal(s) in my physical presence" (OAR 111:6-4).

Electronic Seals and Signatures

An electronic seal must consist of the following as text in the electronic document near the electronic Notary's signature or as a graphic image attached to or logically associated with the signature (ORC 147.6):

— The electronic Notary's name as shown on the Notary's electronic Notary commission;

— The Notary's commission number;

— Commission expiration date;

— Coat of arms of the state within a circle that is at least three-quarters of an inch, but not larger than one inch in diameter surrounded by the words "Notary Public," "Notary Seal" or other words to that effect, and the words "State of Ohio."

An electronic signature (in some instances, referred to as a digital signature) must be:

— Attributed or uniquely linked to the electronic Notary;

— Capable of independent verification;

— Retained under the electronic Notary's exclusive control; and

— Linked to the electronic document to which it relates in such a manner that any subsequent change of the electronic document is detectable.

Online Notarization Rules and Procedures

A Notary that is currently commissioned as an Ohio Notary and is a resident of the state, may apply to act as an online Notary Public during the term of their commission (ORC Sec. 147.63[A]). This authorization permits a Notary to notarize for a remote principal who appears before the Notary via an online notarization with live two-way audio and video communication. Before the online Notary applicant is authorized to perform online Notary acts, he or she must complete a course of instruction from a state-approved education vendor and successfully pass an exam (ORC Sec. 147.63[B][1]). The application must be electronically submitted and include (ORC 147.01)[E]):

— The applicant's full legal name and official Notary Public name to be used in acting as an online Notary Public;

— A description of the technology the applicant intends to use in performing online notarizations;

— A certification that the applicant will comply with the rules adopted under section 147.62 of the Revised Code;

— An electronic mail address of the applicant;

— Any decrypting instructions, keys, codes or software necessary to enable the application to be read;

— Evidence of successful completion of at least two hours of education and testing provided by the authorized education and testing provider;

— A disclosure of any and all license or commission revocations or other professional disciplinary actions taken against the applicant; and

— A fee of $20 to the Secretary of State, which must be paid by credit card.

If the applicant fails the test, he or she may retake the exam but not sooner than 30 days following the date of their last examination, and no later than six months following date of completion of the education program. Should the applicant fail the exam a second time, the applicant must re-start the process with a new application (OAR 111:6-3[A][3]).

For attorneys who are licensed to practice law in the state of Ohio, their online notarization authorization shall be for a period of five years or when the attorney's term of office as a Notary ends, whichever is earlier. For notaries who are not licensed to practice law in the state of Ohio, their authorization to perform online notarizations shall expire when their Notary Public commission expires (OAR 111:6-3[C]).

If at any time the Notary changes either the hardware or the software that the Notary intends to use to carry out online notarizations, then the Notary shall inform the secretary of this intent on a form prescribed by the Secretary of State and submitted electronically. If the Secretary of State determines that the new hardware or software does not meet the standards prescribed in rules under section 147.62 of the Revised Code, then the Secretary may suspend or revoke the Notary's authority to perform online notarizations (ORC 147:63[F][2]).

Online Notary Public Renewal

A nonattorney Notary Public authorized to perform online Notary acts may apply to renew their ability to perform online notarizations within three months of the expiration of their traditional Notary commission (ORC 147:031[C]).

An attorney Notary Public authorized to perform online Notary acts may apply to renew their ability to perform online notarizations within three months of the expiration of their online Notary commission authorization (ORC 147:031[C]).

In order for the Secretary of State to renew a Notary Public's authorization to perform online notarizations, the applicant must electronically submit the application according to the process prescribed by the Secretary of State. The application for renewal shall include (OAR 111:6-3):

— Evidence of successful completion of at least one hour of education as provided an authorized provider;

— The applicant should update any changes to the information provided regarding the description of technology being used in performing online notarizations, decrypting instructions, keys, codes or software necessary to enable the application to be read and a disclosure of any and all license or commission revocations or other professional disciplinary actions taken against the applicant; and

— A fee of $20 dollars, which must be paid by credit card.

For attorneys who are licensed to practice law in the state of Ohio, their authority to perform online notarizations shall be extended for a period of five years or until the attorney's term of office as a Notary ends, whichever is earlier.

For Notaries who are not licensed to practice law in the state of Ohio, their authorization to perform online notarizations shall expire when their traditional Notary Public commission expires (OAR 111:6-3[D][1]).

Technology Requirements for Online Notarial Acts

An online Notary Public must be physically located within the boundaries of Ohio at the time the notarial act takes place; however, the signer may be located anywhere within the territory of the United States (OAR 111:6-5[A]).

Online notarizations must occur with the use of an online notarization system which has two-way live audio and video conference technology and that meets the following requirements (OAR 111:6-5[B]).

The online Notary Public must be able to verify the identity of the remotely located individual at the time the signature is taken by one of the following methods (OAR 111:6-5[B]):

A. The online Notary Public's personal knowledge of the individual;

B. Each of the following:

1. Remote presentation of an unexpired government-issued identification credential that contains the photograph

and signature of the individual to the online Notary Public by means of communication technology;

2. Credential analysis of the identification credential that utilizes public or private data sources to confirm the validity of an identification credential. Note: While the Notary is responsible for ensuring the signer is properly identified, the Notary will be relying on a third party platform provider for these ID services, which must, at a minimum:

   a. Use automated software processes to aid the online Notary Public in verifying the identity of a remotely located individual;

   b. Ensure that the identification credential passes an authenticity test, consistent with sound commercial practices that:

      i. Use appropriate technologies to confirm the integrity of visual, physical, or cryptographic security features;

      ii. Use appropriate technologies to confirm that the identification credential is not fraudulent or inappropriately modified;

      iii. Use information held or published by the issuing source or an authoritative source, as available, to confirm the validity of identification credential details; and

      iv. Provide output of the authenticity test to the online Notary Public;

   c. Enable the online Notary Public to visually compare for consistency:

      i. The information and photograph on the presented credential, and

      ii. The remotely located individual as viewed by the online Notary Public in real time through communication technology;

d. Require a government-issued identification credential that:

   i. Is an unexpired government-issued identification credential that contains the photograph and signature of the individual; and

   ii. May be imaged, photographed, and video recorded under applicable state and federal law; and

   iii. Can be subjected to credential analysis.

e. Include an image capture procedure that confirms that:

   i. The remotely located individual is in possession of the credential at the time of the notarial act;

   ii. Credential images submitted for credential analysis have not been manipulated; and

   iii. Credential images match the credential in the possession of the remotely located individual; and

f. Require the captured image of the identification credential to:

   i. Be of sufficient image resolution to perform credential analysis in accordance with the requirements of this subsection;

   ii. Be of sufficient image resolution to enable visual inspection of the credential by the Notary Public; and

   iii. Include all images necessary to perform visual inspection and credential analysis in accordance with the requirements of this subsection, including the identity page of any passport and the front and back images of any identification card.

3. Identity proofing performed by means of a knowledge-based authentication. Note: While the Notary is responsible for ensuring the signer is properly identified, the Notary will be relying on a third party platform provider that meets the following requirements:

   a. Each remotely located individual must answer a quiz consisting of a minimum of five questions related to the remotely located individual's personal history or identity, formulated from public or private data sources;

   b. Each question must have a minimum of five possible answer choices;

   c. At least 80% of the questions must be answered correctly;

   d. All questions must be answered within two minutes;

   e. If the remotely located individual fails the first attempt, the individual may retake the quiz two times within 48 hours;

   f. During a retake of the quiz, a minimum of 40% of the prior questions must be replaced;

   g. If the remotely located individual fails the second attempt, the individual is not permitted to retry with the same Notary or the same third person providing the identity proofing service within 24 hours of the second failed attempt; and

   h. The online Notary Public must not be able to see or record the questions or answers.

4. Oath or affirmation of a single credible witness who personally knows the individual and either is personally known to the online Notary Public or who is identified by the online Notary Public under the rules of this section.

The online notarization system used must meet the following criteria (OAR 111:6-5[B][6]):

— The persons communicating must simultaneously see and speak to one another.

— The signal transmission must be live, real time.

— The signal transmission must be secure from interception or access by anyone other than the persons communicating.

— The technology must provide sufficient audio clarity and video resolution to enable the Notary to communicate with the signer and utilize the permissible signer identification.

— The system must provide confirmation that the electronic document presented is the same as the electronic document notarized.

— The system must allow for the affixation of the notarial certificate, signature and seal.

— The system must allow for viewing the notarial certificate, signature and seal.

— The system must provide a method for determining if the electronic document has been altered after the electronic notarial seal has been affixed and the electronic notarial act has been completed.

— The system must provide a method of generating a paper copy of the document including the notarial certificate, signature and seal and any other document associated with the execution of the notarial act.

If the signer or online Notary Public must exit the audio-video communication session, the audio-video communication link is broken, or the resolution or quality of the transmission becomes such that the electronic Notary Public believes the process has been compromised and cannot be completed, the identity authentication process and any incomplete online notarial acts must be started from the beginning (OAR 111:6-5[C]).

Online Notarization Certificate Forms

For electronic notarial acts performed by an online Notary using audio-video communication for a principal not in the online

Notary's physical presence, the Notary certificate forms provided in section 147.55 of the Revised Code may be used if the forms include this statement or something similar: "This certificate pertains to an electronic notarial act performed with the principal(s) appearing online using audio-video communication." (OAR 111:6-4).

Electronic Journals

An online Notary Public must keep, maintain and protect an electronic journal of all notarial acts that took place during the term of the Notary Public's authorization to perform online notarizations. For every online notarization, the electronic journal must include all elements required by section 147.65(B) of the Revised Code and comply with security measures as required by section 147.65(C) and (D) of the Revised Code.

For every online notarization, the online Notary Public must record the following information in the electronic journal (ORC Sec.147.65[B]):

— date and time of notarial act;

— type of notarial act;

— title or a description of the record being notarized, if any;

— electronic signature of each principal;

— if identification of the principal is based on satisfactory evidence of identity, a description of the evidence relied upon, including the date of issuance or expiration of any identification credential presented;

— if identification of the principal is based on a credible witness or witnesses, the name of the witness or witnesses;

— if the notarization was not performed at the online Notary Public's business address, the address where the notarization was performed;

— a description of the online notarization system used;

— fee, if any, charged by the Notary;

— name of the jurisdiction in which the principal was located at the time of the online notarization

— recording upon which the identification of the principal is based

An online Notary Public must not record a Social Security number in the electronic journal (ORC Sec.147.65[C]).

Any system used to store the electronic journal must also allow entries to be made, viewed, printed out and copied by an online Notary only after access is obtained by at least one factor of authentication such as a password, biometric verification, token, or other form of authentication. It must also have a backup system in place to provide a duplicate electronic journal of notarial acts as a precaution in the event of loss of the original record (ORC 147.65[D]).

Any system used to store the electronic journal must not allow an entry to be deleted or altered in content or sequence by the electronic Notary or any other person after a record of the electronic notarization is entered and stored (ORC 147.65 [D][5]).

Any system used to store the electronic journal must allow the online Notary Public sole control of the electronic journal and the recording of the electronic notarial act using audio-visual communication, subject to the authorized access granted by the Notary (ORC 147.65 [D][5]).

An online Notary Public must create and maintain a recording of the audio-video communication of each online notarization as well as a backup of the electronic journal and audio-video recordings (ORC Sec.147.65[D][3-4]).

The online Notary may use a third party to keep and store electronic journals and recordings. The Secretary of State must be made aware of the location of these electronic journals and recordings (ORC Sec.147.65[D][5][F][2]). At the end of the online Notary's commission, the electronic journal must be transmitted to the Secretary of State or a repository approved by the Secretary of State. The Secretary of State or the repository must maintain the electronic journal for a period of 10 years (ORC Sec.147.65[F][2]).

Online Notarization Fees

The fee charged includes receiving evidence of the signer's identity, administering an oath or affirmation, if applicable, and applying the signature, notarial certificate and seal to the document. A Notary Public may charge the following fees (ORC 147.08):

— Up to twenty-five dollars per document for an online notarization.

— A Notary may charge a reasonable travel fee, as agreed to by the Notary and the signer prior to the notarial act. ■

Ohio Laws Pertaining to Notaries Public

Reprinted on the following pages is the complete text of the enacted laws affecting Notaries and notarial acts, drawn from the Ohio Revised Code.

OHIO REVISED CODE
CHAPTER 147
NOTARIES PUBLIC AND COMMISSIONERS

147.01. Appointment and commission of notaries public - notary public for state.

(A) The secretary of state may appoint and commission as notaries public as many persons who meet the qualifications of division (B) of this section as the secretary of state considers necessary.

(B) In order for a person to qualify to be appointed and commissioned as a notary public, the person shall demonstrate to the secretary of state that the person satisfies all of the following:

(1) The person has attained the age of eighteen years.

(a) Except as provided in division (B)(2)(b) of this section, the person is a legal resident of this state.

(b) The person is not a legal resident of this state, but is an attorney admitted to the practice of law in this state by the Ohio supreme court, and has the person's principal place of business or the person's primary practice in this state.

(3)(a) Except as provided in division (B)(3)(b) of this section, the person has submitted a criminal records check report completed within the preceding six months in accordance with section 147.022 of the Revised Code demonstrating that the applicant has not been convicted of or pleaded guilty or no contest to a disqualifying offense, or any offense under an existing or former law of this state, any other state, or the United States that is substantially equivalent to such a disqualifying offense.

(b) An attorney admitted to the practice of law in this state shall not be required to submit a criminal records check when applying to be appointed a notary public.

(4)(a) Except as provided in divisions (B)(4)(b) and (c) of this section, the person has successfully completed an educational program and passed a test administered by the entities authorized by the secretary of state as required under section 147.021 of the Revised Code.

(b) An attorney who is commissioned as a notary public in this state prior to the effective date of this amendment shall not be required to complete an education program or pass a test as required in division (B)(4)(a) of this section.

(c) Any attorney who applies to become commissioned as a notary public in this state after the effective date of this amendment shall not be required to pass a test as required in division (B)(4)(a) of this section, but shall be required to complete an education program required by that division.

(C) A notary public shall be appointed and commissioned as a notary public for the state. The secretary of state may revoke a commission issued to a notary public upon presentation of satisfactory evidence of official misconduct or incapacity.

(D) The secretary of state shall oversee the processing of notary public applications and shall issue all notary public commissions. The secretary of state shall oversee the creation and maintenance of the online database of notaries public commissioned in this state pursuant to section 147.051 of the Revised Code. The secretary of state may perform all other duties as required by this section. The entities authorized by the secretary of state pursuant to section 147.021 or 147.63 of the Revised Code shall administer the educational program and required test or course of instruction and examination, as applicable.

(E) All submissions to the secretary of state for receiving and renewing commissions, or notifications made under section 147.05 of the Revised Code, shall be done electronically.

Effective Date: 09-20-2019

Sec. 147.011. Definitions. As used in this chapter:

(A) "Acknowledgment" means a notarial act in which the signer of the notarized document acknowledges all of the following:

(1) That the signer has signed the document;

(2) That the signer understands the document;

(3) That the signer is aware of the consequences of executing the document by signing it.

(B) "Criminal records check" has the same meaning as in section 109.572 of the Revised Code.

(C) "Disqualifying offense" means a crime of moral turpitude as defined in section 4776.10 of the Revised Code and a violation of a provision of Chapter 2913. of the Revised Code.

(D) "Jurat" means a notarial act in which both of the following are met:

(1) The signer of the notarized document is required to give an oath or affirmation that the statement in the notarized document is true and correct;

(2) The signer signs the notarized document in the presence of a notary public.

(E) "Notarial certificate" means the part of, or attachment to, a document that is completed by the notary public and upon which the notary public places the notary public's signature and seal.

Sec. 021. Education and Testing. (A)(1) Except as provided in division (B)(4) of section 147.01 of the Revised Code, no person shall be appointed as a notary public unless that person has completed an educational program related to the requirements of this chapter and passed a test demonstrating knowledge of such requirements.

(2) The secretary of state may authorize that such a program be completed online.

(B) The secretary of state shall adopt, in rules under Chapter 119. of the Revised Code, standards and curricula for the educational program required under this section. The rules shall address all of the following:

(1) The entities authorized to administer the educational program and the required test, which shall include the following entities that meet the minimum requirements established by the secretary of state:

(a) Those entities providing notary public educational programming and testing services prior to the effective date of this section;

(b) Another entity that has a business relationship with an entity described in division (B)(1) (a) of this section.

(2) The standards and curricula of the program, which shall be established in coordination with the entities authorized to administer the program and the required test and shall include all of the following:

(a) The terms of notary commission;

(b) How to renew a commission;

(c) The conditions under which a commission may be revoked;

(d) What constitutes a legal notarial act;

(e) The manner of taking depositions;

(f) The taking of an acknowledgment;

(g) The administration of a jurat.

(3) The provisions and content of the required test, which shall be established in coordination with the entities authorized to administer the educational program and required test.

Sec. 147.022. Criminal Records Check. (A)(1) The secretary of state shall require each applicant for a notary commission, other than an attorney licensed to practice law in this state, to complete a criminal records check.

(2) The secretary shall not accept an application for a notary commission that includes the report of a criminal records check that is more than six months old.

(B) The secretary of state shall provide to each person applying for a notary commission, other than an attorney admitted to the practice of law in this state, information about accessing, completing, and forwarding to the superintendent of the bureau of criminal identification and investigation the form prescribed pursuant to division (C)(1) of section 109.572 of the Revised Code and the standard impression sheet to obtain fingerprint impressions prescribed pursuant to division (C)(2) of that section.

(C) Each person requesting a criminal records check under this section shall pay to the bureau of criminal identification and investigation the fee prescribed pursuant to division (C)(3) of section 109.572 of the Revised Code.

(D) The report of any criminal records check conducted by the bureau of criminal identification and investigation in accordance with section 109.572 of the Revised Code and pursuant to a request made under this section is not a public record for the purposes of section 149.43 of the Revised Code and shall not be made available to any person other than the following:

(1) The person who is the subject of the criminal records check or the person's representative;

(2) The secretary of state and the staff of the secretary of state;

(3) A court, hearing officer, or other necessary individual involved in a case dealing with a commission denial resulting from the criminal records check.

(E) The secretary of state shall deny a notary commission application if, after receiving the information and notification required by this section, a person subject the criminal records check requirement fails to do either of the following:

(1) Access, complete, or forward to the superintendent of the bureau of criminal identification and investigation the form prescribed pursuant to division (C)(1) of section 109.572 of the Revised Code or the standard impression sheet prescribed pursuant to division (C)(2) of that section; (2) Submit the completed report of the criminal records check to the secretary of state. Effective Date: 09-20-2019

147.02. Certificate of qualifications.

(A) Before the appointment of a notary public is made, the applicant shall produce to the secretary of state a certificate from a judge or justice of the court of common pleas, court of appeals, or supreme court that contains the following:

(1) A statement that the applicant is of good moral character;

(2) If the applicant is not an attorney admitted to the practice of law in this state by the Ohio supreme court, a statement that the applicant is a citizen of the county in which the applicant resides;

(3) If the applicant is an attorney admitted to the practice of law in this state by the Ohio supreme court, a statement that the applicant is possessed of sufficient qualifications and ability to discharge the duties of the office of notary public.

(B) No judge or justice shall issue a certificate required by division (A) of this section until the judge or justice is satisfied from personal knowledge that the applicant possesses the qualifications necessary to a proper discharge of the duties of the office or until the applicant has passed an examination under any rules that the judge or justice may prescribe.

(C) If the applicant is a citizen of this state who is an attorney admitted to the practice of law in this state by the Ohio supreme court, the judge or justice also shall certify this fact in the certification required by division (A) of this section.

(D) If the applicant is not a citizen of this state but is an attorney who is admitted to the practice of law in this state by the Ohio supreme court and whose principal place of business or primary practice is in this state, the judge or justice also shall certify these facts in the certification required by division (A) of this section.

(E) For the purposes of sections 147.03, 147.04, 147.05, and 147.13 of the Revised Code, the county in which an attorney who is not a citizen of this state and who is a notary public has the attorney's principal place of business or the attorney's primary practice shall be deemed the county in which the attorney resides.

Effective Date: 06-06-2001

147.03. Term of office - oath - removal for violating oath.

Each notary public, except an attorney admitted to the practice of law in this state by the Ohio supreme court, shall hold office for the term of five years unless the commission is revoked. An attorney admitted to the practice of law in this state by the Ohio supreme court shall hold office as a notary public as long as the attorney is a resident of this state or has the attorney's principal place of business or primary practice in this state, the attorney is in good standing before the Ohio supreme court, and the commission is not revoked. Before entering upon the duties of office, a notary public shall take and subscribe an oath to be endorsed on the notary public's commission.

A notary public who violates the oath of office required by this section shall be removed from office by thesecretary of state, upon complaint filed and substantiated bythe secretary of state. The person so removed shall be ineligible for reappointment to the office of notary public.

Effective Date: 09-20-2019

Sec. 147.031. Renewal of Commission.

(A)(1) Except as provided in division (A)(2) of this section, a commission for a notary public appointed prior to the effective date of this section shall remain valid until that commission's expiration date.

(2) A commission issued to an attorney shall be governed by section 147.03 of the Revised Code.

(B) A commission that is set to expire as described in section 147.03 of the Revised Code or as in division (A) of this section shall not be renewed unless the notary submits to the secretary of state through the entities authorized in section 147.021 of the Revised Code all of the following:

(1) A new criminal records check report as required under division (B)(3) of section 147.01 of the Revised Code;

(2) A fee of not more than sixty dollars, set by the secretary of state in a rule adopted under Chapter 119. of the Revised Code;

(3) An application for renewal on a form prescribed by the secretary.

(C) A notary public may apply to renew the notary's commission beginning three months prior to the expiration date of the commission.

(D) If the notary public's commission expires before the notary submits the application for renewal, the secretary of state shall not renew that expired commission but shall permit the person to apply for a new notary commission.

Sec. 147.032. Investigations; Penalties. (A)(1) If the secretary of state believes that a violation of this chapter has occurred, the secretary of state may investigate such violations.

(2) The secretary of state may investigate possible violations of this chapter upon a signed complaint from any person.

(B) The secretary of state may hold a disciplinary hearing if the secretary of state determines a hearing to be appropriate after an investigation conducted under division (A) of this section.

(C) After holding an administrative hearing and concluding that a violation of this chapter has occurred, the secretary of state may do any of the following:

(1) Revoke the notary public's commission;

(2) Suspend the notary public's commission for a specified period of time or until fulfillment of a condition, such as retraining, or both.

(3) Issue a letter of admonition that shall be placed in the notary public's record.

(D) A person whose notary commission has been revoked may not apply for a subsequent notary commission.

(E) The secretary of state may adopt rules under Chapter 119. of the Revised Code to set forth procedures for investigations and hearings regarding violations of this chapter and disciplinary actions taken.

(F) The secretary of state may establish an advisory board to meet as the secretary of state considers necessary to discuss matters related to notary law and procedures.
Effective Date: 09-20-2019

147.04. Seal and register.

Before entering upon the discharge of official duties, a notary public shall obtain a seal of a notary public. The seal shall consist of the coat of arms of the state within a circle that is at least three-quarters of an inch, but not larger than one inch in diameter and shall be surrounded by the words "notary public," "notarial seal," or words to that effect, the name of the notary public, and the words "State of Ohio." The seal may be of either a type that will stamp ink onto a document or one that will emboss it. The name of the notary public may, instead of appearing on the seal, be printed, typewritten, or stamped in legible, printed letters near the notary public's signature on each document signed by the notary public.

Effective Date: 09-20-2019

Sec. 147.041. Persons Commissioned Prior to September 20, 2019.

A person commissioned as a notary public prior to the effective date of this section may continue to use a seal that met the requirements of section 147.04 of the Revised Code and that was in that person's possession before that date.

Effective Date: 09-20-2019

147.05 Recordkeeping; Change of Address; Notice of Resignation or Conviction of Disqualifying Offense.

(A) The secretary of state shall maintain a record of the commissions of each notary public appointed and commissioned by the secretary of state under this chapter and make a proper index to that record.

The governor's office shall transfer to the secretary of state's office, on or after June 6, 2001, the record of notaries public formerly kept by the governor's office under section 107.10 of the Revised Code. The secretary of state's office shall maintain that record together with the record and index of commissions of notaries public required by this division.

(B) If a notary public legally changes the notary public's name or address after having been commissioned as a notary public, the notary public shall notify the secretary of state within thirty days after the name or address change. Such a notification shall be on a form prescribed by the secretary of state.

(C) A notary who resigns the person's commission shall deliver to the secretary of state, on a form prescribed by the secretary of state, a written notice indicating the effective date of resignation.

(D)(1) A notary shall inform the secretary of state of being convicted of or pleading guilty or no contest to any disqualifying offense, as defined in section 147.011 of the Revised Code, or any offense under an existing or former law of this state, any other state, or the United States that is substantially equivalent to such a disqualifying offense during the term of the notary's commission.

(2) The secretary of state shall revoke the commission of any person who is convicted of or pleads guilty or no contest to a disqualifying offense, including an attorney licensed to practice law in this state.

Effective Date: 09-20-2019

Sec. 147.051. Database of Notaries. The secretary of state shall maintain a database of notaries public on a publicly accessible web site. The web site shall provide all of the following information in relation to each notary public:

(A) A verification of the authority and good standing of the individual to perform notarial acts;

(B) Whether the notary is registered to perform online notarizations, as defined in section 147.60 of the Revised Code;

(C) A description of any administrative or disciplinary action taken against the notary.

Effective Date: 09-20-2019

147.06. Certified copy of commission as evidence - fee.

Upon application, the secretary of state shall make a certified copy of a notary public commission and the endorsements on the commission. The certified copy shall be prima-facie evidence of the matters and facts contained in it. For each certified copy of a notary public commission, the secretary of state shall be entitled to receive a fee of five dollars.

Effective Date: 09-20-2019

147.07. Powers - jurisdiction.

A notary public may, throughout the state, administer oaths required or authorized by law, take and certify depositions, and take and certify acknowledgments of deeds, mortgages, liens, powers of attorney, and other instruments of writing. In taking depositions, a notary public shall have the power that is by law vested in judges of county courts to compel the attendance of witnesses and punish them for refusing to testify. Sheriffs and constables are required to serve and return all process issued by notaries public in the taking of depositions.

Effective Date: 09-20-2019

147.08. Fees.

A notary public is entitled to the following fees:

(1) Up to five dollars for any notarial act that is not an online notarization;

(2) For an online notarization, up to twenty-five dollars.

(B) A notary charging the fee authorized under division (A) (2) of this section shall not also charge the fee authorized under division (A)(1) of this section.

(C) The fees charged under division (A) of this section shall not be calculated on a per signature basis.

(D) In addition to the fees authorized under division (A) of this section, a notary may charge a reasonable travel fee, as agreed to by the notary and the principal prior to the notarial act.

(E) The secretary of state may adopt rules under Chapter 119. of the Revised Code to increase the fees authorized under this section.

Effective Date: 09-20-2019

147.09 Protests are evidence. REPEALED on September 20, 2019.

The instrument of protest of a notary public appointed and qualified under the laws of this state or of any other state or territory of the United States, accompanying a bill of exchange or promissory note, which has been protested by such notary public for nonacceptance or for nonpayment constitutes prima-facie evidence of the facts therein certified. Such instrument may be contradicted by other evidence.

Effective Date: 10-01-1953

147.10 Notary public acting after commission expires.

No notary public shall do or perform any act as a notary public knowing that the notary public's term of office has expired or that the notary public has resigned the notary public's commission.

Effective Date: 10-01-1953; 06-30-2005

147.11 Forfeiture.

A person appointed notary public who performs any act as such after the expiration of the person's term of office or after the person resigns the person's commission, knowing that the person's term has expired or that the person has resigned, shall forfeit not more than five hundred dollars, to be recovered by an action in the name of the state. Such act shall render the person ineligible for reappointment.

Effective Date: 10-01-1953; 06-30-2005

147.12 Acts done by notary public after term valid.

An official act done by a notary public after the expiration of the notary public's term of office or after the notary public resigns the notary public's commission is as valid as if done during the notary public's term of office.

Effective Date: 10-01-1953; 06-30-2005

147.13 Removal for receiving excess fees.

A notary public who charges or receives for an act or service done or rendered by the notary public a fee greater than the amount prescribed by law, or who dishonestly or unfaithfully discharges any official duties as notary public, shall be removed from office by thesecretary of state, upon complaint filed and substantiated by the secretary of state. The person so removed shall be ineligible for reappointment to the office of notary public.

Effective Date: 09-20-2019

147.14 Removal from office for certifying affidavit without administering oath.

No notary public shall certify to the affidavit of a person without administering the appropriate oath or affirmation to the person. A notary public who violates this section shall be removed from office by the secretary of state. The person so removed shall be ineligible to reappointment for a period of three years.

Effective Date: 09-20-2019

Sec. 147.141. Prohibited Acts. (A) A notary public shall not do any of the following:

(1) Perform a notarial act with regard to a record or document executed by the notary;

(2) Notarize the notary's own signature;

(3) Take the notary's own deposition;

(4) Perform a notarial act if the notary has a conflict of interest with regard to the transaction in question;

(5) Certify that a document is either of the following:

(a) An original document;

(b) A true copy of another record.

(6) Use a name or initial in signing certificates other than that by which the notary public is commissioned;

(7) Sign notarial certificates using a facsimile signature stamp unless the notary public has a physical disability that limits or prohibits the notary's ability to make a written signature and unless the notary has first submitted written notice to the secretary of state with an example of the facsimile signature stamp;

(8) Affix the notary's signature to a blank form of an affidavit or certificate of acknowledgment and deliver that form to another person with the intent that it be used as an affidavit or acknowledgment;

(9) Take the acknowledgment of, or administer an oath or affirmation to, a person who the notary public knows to have been adjudicated mentally incompetent by a court of competent jurisdiction, if the acknowledgment or oath or affirmation necessitates the exercise of a right that has been removed;

(10) Notarize a signature on a document if it appears that the person is mentally incapable of understanding the nature and effect of the document at the time of notarization;

(11) Alter anything in a written instrument after it has been signed by anyone;

(12) Amend or alter a notarial certificate after the notarization is complete;

(13) Notarize a signature on a document if the document is incomplete or blank;

(14) Notarize a signature on a document if it appears that the signer may be unduly influenced or coerced so as to be restricted from or compromised in exercising the person's own free will when signing the document;

(15) Take an acknowledgment of execution in lieu of an oath or affirmation if an oath or affirmation is required;

(16) Determine the validity of a power of attorney document or any other form designating a representative capacity, such as trustee, authorized officer, agent, personal representative, or guardian, unless that notary is an attorney licensed to practice law in this state.

(B) Division (A)(5) of this section shall not be construed as prohibiting a notary from notarizing the signature of a holder of a document on a written statement certifying that the document is a true copy of an original document.

(C) As used in this section, "conflict of interest" means either of the following:

(1) The notary has a direct financial or other interest in the transaction in question, excluding the fees authorized under this chapter.

(2) The notary is named, individually or as a grantor, grantee, mortgagor, mortgagee, trustor, trustee, beneficiary, vendor, lessor, or lessee, or as a party in some other capacity to the transaction. Effective Date: 09-20-2019

Sec. 147.142. Advisement as Immigration Consultant; Other Prohibited Acts. (A) A notary public who is not a licensed attorney in this state shall not represent or advertise himself or herself as an immigration consultant or an expert in immigration matters.

(B) A notary public who is not a licensed attorney in this state shall not do any of the following:

(1) Provide any service that constitutes the unauthorized practice of law in violation of section 4705.07 of the Revised Code;

(2) State or imply that the notary is an attorney licensed to practice law in this state;

(3) Solicit or accept compensation to prepare documents for or otherwise represent the interest of another person in a judicial or administrative proceeding, including a proceeding relating to immigration to the United States, United States citizenship, or related matters;

(4) Solicit or accept compensation to obtain relief of any kind on behalf of another from any officer, agency, or employee of this state or of the United States;

(5) Use the phrase "notario" or "notario publico" to advertise the services of a notary public, whether by sign, pamphlet, stationery, or other written communication, or by radio, television, or other non - written communication. Effective Date: 09-20-2019

147.32 Representatives of veterans' organizations may be appointed as commissioners of the state.

Representatives of the United Spanish War Veterans, The Disabled American Veterans, The American Legion, Veterans of Foreign Wars of the United States, and other congressionally chartered veterans' organizations, who are recognized as such representatives by the administrator of the veterans' administration, and who are engaged in the preparation and prosecution of claims of veterans and their dependents before the rating agencies of the veterans' administration within the state, may be appointed as commissioners of the state. Such commissioners shall continue in office for a term of three years. Each of such commissioners shall, before performing any of his duties, take and subscribe to an oath of office before a judge of a court of record within this state. Such oath, with his signature thereto and an impression of his seal of office and his residence address, shall forthwith be transmitted by him to the governor, and filed by the governor in the office of the secretary of state.

Each of such commissioners shall procure and employ a seal of the dimensions and inscription set forth and prescribed for notaries public, in section 147.04 of the Revised Code, except that the words shall be: "Commissioner of the State of Ohio for Veterans' Affairs."

Such commissioners may, without fee and within the state, administer oaths, take acknowledgments, and attest the execution of any instruments of writing only in connection with or used before the veterans' administration.

Effective Date: 10-14-1963

147.33 to 147.36 [Repealed].

Effective Date: 10-14-1963

147.37 Fees for commissions.

(A) The secretary of state shall establish a fee of not more than one hundred fifty dollars to be paid by each person receiving a commission as notary public.

(B) The notary public shall remit the fee to the authorized entity that administered the educational program and test required by section 147.021 of the Revised Code. The notary public shall remit to the secretary of state the portion of that fee specified pursuant to division (C)(2) of this section.

(C) The secretary of state shall adopt rules in accordance with Chapter 119. of the Revised Code to do all of the following:

(1) Establish the amount of the fee authorized by division (A) of this section;

(2) Establish the portion of the fee, not to exceed fifteen dollars, that the notary public is required to remit to the secretary of state;

(3) Establish the portion of the fee that a notary who is an attorney shall remit to the entity that administered the educational program a fee of fifteen dollars to the secretary of state.

Effective Date: 09-26-2003

147.371 Duplicate commission.

(A) Upon receipt of a fee of two dollars and an affidavit that the original commission of a notary public has been lost or destroyed, a duplicate commission as notary public shall be issued by the secretary of state.

(B) Upon receipt of a fee of two dollars and the properly completed, prescribed form for a name and address change under division (B) of section 147.05 of the Revised Code, the secretary of state shall issue a duplicate commission as a notary public.

Effective Date: 06-06-2001; 06-30-2005; 09-20-2019

147.38 [Repealed].

Effective Date: 05-31-1988

147.39 Prior notarial acts by armed forces officers valid.

Any acknowledgment or proof of execution of a deed, mortgage, lease, power of attorney, or other instrument that was taken, and any other notarial act that was performed, by a commissioned officer in active service with the armed forces of the United States for a person who was a member of the armed forces of the United States, for a person who was accompanying the armed forces of the United States, or for a person who was a dependent of either such category of persons, and that was taken or performed between January 1, 1941, and January 1, 1974, in conformity with the provisions of a prior statute that then was in effect is as valid as if the acknowledgment, proof of execution, or other notarial act was performed in conformity with the provisions of sections 147.51 to 147.58 of the Revised Code.

Effective Date: 05-31-1988

147.40 Manner of taking depositions.

Depositions taken in pursuance of sections 147.07 and 147.51 to 147.58 of the Revised Code by a person described in division (D) of section 147.51 of the Revised Code shall be taken on written interrogatories, on a written notice being given by the party desiring to take such depositions, which notice shall contain the names of the parties plaintiff and defendant, the court or tribunal in which the action is pending, the number of the regiment or battalion to which the witness belongs, and the names of the witnesses. The notice shall be served upon the adverse party, or his agent or attorney of record, or left at his usual place of abode, with a copy of the interrogatories, at least twenty days prior to the taking of such depositions. If the party on whom such notice is served desires to file cross-interrogatories, a copy of them shall be served on the adverse party, or his agent or attorney of record, or left at his usual place of abode, within six days after the notice of taking depositions has been served, and the party giving the notice to take depositions, shall forward with his notice and interrogatories, the cross-interrogatories so served on him; and neither party, by himself, or his agent or attorney, shall be present at the time of taking such depositions.

Effective Date: 05-31-1988

147.51 Notarial acts.

For the purposes of sections 147.51 to 147.58 of the Revised Code, "notarial acts" means acts which the laws and regulations of this state authorize notaries public of this state to perform, including the administration of oaths and affirmations, taking proof of execution and acknowledgment of instruments, attesting documents, and executing a jurat.

Notarial acts may be performed outside this state for use in this state with the same effect as if performed by a notary public of this state by the following persons authorized pursuant to the laws and regulations of other governments, in addition to any other persons authorized by the laws and regulations of this state:

(A) A notary public authorized to perform notarial acts in the place in which the act is performed;

(B) A judge, clerk, or deputy clerk of any court of record in the place in which the notarial act is performed;

(C) An officer of the foreign service of the United States, a consular agent, or any other person authorized by regulation of the United States department of state to perform notarial acts in the place in which the act is performed;

(D) A commissioned officer in active service with the armed forces of the United States and any other person authorized by regulation of the armed forces to perform notarial acts if the notarial act is performed for one of the following or for a dependent of one of the following:

(1) A member of the merchant marines of the United States;

(2) A member of the armed forces of the United States;

(3) Any other person serving with or accompanying the armed forces of the United States;

(E) Any other person authorized to perform notarial acts in the place in which the act is performed.

Effective Date: 01-01-1974

147.52. Notarial acts by authorized person.

(A) If the notarial act is performed by any of the persons described in divisions (A) to (D) of section 147.51 of the Revised Code, other than a person authorized to perform notarial acts by the laws or regulations of a foreign country, the signature, rank, or title and serial number, if any, of the person are sufficient proof of the authority of a holder of that rank or title to perform the act. Further proof of his authority is not required.

(B) If the notarial act is performed by a person authorized by the laws or regulations of a foreign country to perform the act, there is sufficient proof of the authority of that person to act if:

(1) Either a foreign service officer of the United States residing in the country in which the act is performed or a diplomatic or consular officer of the foreign country residing in the United States certifies that a person holding that office is authorized to perform the act;

(2) The official seal of the person performing the notarial act is affixed to the document; or

(3) The title and indication of authority to perform notarial acts of the person appears either in a digest of foreign law or in a list customarily used as a source of such information.

(C) If the notarial act is performed by a person other than one described in divisions (A) and (B) of this section, there is sufficient proof of the authority of that person to act if the clerk of a court of record in the place in which the notarial act is performed certifies to the official character of that person and to his authority to perform the notarial act.

(D) The signature and title of the person performing the act are prima-facie evidence that he is a person with the designated title and that the signature is genuine.

Effective Date: 06-13-1975

147.53. Taking an acknowledgment.

The person taking an acknowledgment shall certify that:

(A) The person acknowledging appeared before him and acknowledged he executed the instrument;

(B) The person acknowledging was known to the person taking the acknowledgment, or that the person taking the acknowledgment had satisfactory evidence that the person acknowledging was the person described in and who executed the instrument.

Effective Date: 01-01-1974

147.54. Recognized certificate of acknowledgment.

The form of a certificate of acknowledgment used by a person whose authority is recognized under section 147.51 of the Revised Code shall be accepted in this state if:

(A) The certificate is in a form prescribed by the laws or regulations of this state;

(B) The certificate is in a form prescribed by the laws or regulations applicable in the place in which the acknowledgment is taken; or

(C) The certificate contains the words "acknowledged before me," or their substantial equivalent.

Effective Date: 06-13-1975

147.541 Acknowledged before me defined.

The words "acknowledged before me" means that:

(A) The person acknowledging appeared before the person taking the acknowledgment;

(B) He acknowledged he executed the instrument;

(C) In the case of:

(1) A natural person, he executed the instrument for the purposes therein stated;

(2) A corporation, the officer or agent acknowledged he held the position or title set forth in the instrument and certificate, he signed the instrument on behalf of the corporation by proper authority, and the instrument was the act of the corporation for the purpose therein stated;

(3) A partnership, the partner or agent acknowledged he signed the instrument on behalf of the partnership by proper authority and he executed the instrument as the act of the partnership for the purposes therein stated;

(4) A person acknowledging as principal by an attorney in fact, he executed the instrument by proper authority as the act of the principal for the purposes therein stated;

(5) A person acknowledging as a public officer, trustee, administrator, guardian, or other representative, he signed the instrument by proper authority and he executed the instrument in the capacity and for the purposes therein stated; and

(D) The person taking the acknowledgment either knew or had satisfactory evidence that the person acknowledging was the person named in the instrument or certificate.

Effective Date: 06-13-1975

Sec. 147.542. Notarial Certificates. (A) A notary public shall provide a completed notarial certificate for every notarial act the notary public performs.

(B) For an acknowledgment and a jurat, the corresponding notarial certificate shall indicate the type of notarization being performed.

(C) If a notarial certificate incorrectly indicates the type of notarization performed, the notary public shall provide a correct certificate at no charge to the person signing in question.

(D)(1) An acknowledgment certificate shall clearly state that no oath or affirmation was administered to the signer with regard to the notarial act.

(2) A jurat certificate shall clearly state that an oath or affirmation was administered to the signer with regard to the notarial act.

(E) (1) A notary public shall not use an acknowledgment certificate with regard to a notarial act in which an oath or affirmation has been administered.

(2) A notary public shall not use a jurat certificate with regard to a notarial act in which an oath or affirmation has not been administered.

(F) A certificate required under this section may be provided through any of the following means:

(1) Preprinting on a notarial document;

(2) Ink stamp;

(3) Handwritten note;

(4) A separate, attached document.

(G) A notarial certificate shall show all of the following information:

(1) The state and county venue where the notarization is being performed;

(2) The wording of the acknowledgment or jurat in question;

(3) The date on which the notarial act was performed;

(4) The signature of the notary, exactly as shown on the notary's commission;

(5) The notary's printed name, displayed below the notary's signature or inked stamp;

(6) The notary's notarial seal and commission expiration date;

(7) If an electronic document was signed in the physical presence of a notary and notarized pursuant to section 147.591 of the Revised Code, or if an online notarization was performed pursuant to sections 147.60 to 147.66 of the Revised Code, the certificate shall include a statement to that effect.

(H) A notary public may explain to a signer the difference between an acknowledgment and a jurat, but shall not, unless that notary is an attorney, advise the person on the type of notarial act that best suits a situation.

147.55 Statutory short forms of acknowledgment.

Notwithstanding section 147.542 of the Revised Code, the forms of acknowledgment set forth in this section may be used and are sufficient for their respective purposes under any section of the Revised Code. The forms shall be known as "statutory short forms of acknowledgment" and may be referred to by that name. The authorization of the forms in this section does not preclude the use of other forms.

"(A) For an individual acting in the individual's own right:

> "State of............................
> County of...........................
>
> The foregoing instrument was acknowledged before me this (date) by (name of person acknowledging).
>
> (Signature of person taking acknowledgment)
> (Title or rank)"

(B) "For a corporation:

"State of............................
County of............................

The foregoing instrument was acknowledged before me this (date) by (name of officer or agent, title of officer or agent) of (name of corporation acknowledging), a (state or place of incorporation) corporation, on behalf of the corporation.

(Signature of person taking acknowledgment)
(Title or rank)"

(C) "For a partnership:

"State of............................
County of............................

The foregoing instrument was acknowledged before me this (date) by (name of acknowledging partner or agent), partner (or agent) on behalf of (name of partnership), a partnership.

(Signature of person taking acknowledgment)
(Title or rank)"

(D) "For an individual acting as principal by an attorney in fact:

"State of............................
County of............................

The foregoing instrument was acknowledged before me this (date) by (name of attorney in fact) as attorney in fact on behalf of (name of principal).

(Signature of person taking acknowledgment)
(Title or rank)"

(E) "By any public officer, trustee, or personal representative:

"State of............................
County of............................

The foregoing instrument was acknowledged before me this (date) by (name and title of position).

(Signature of person taking acknowledgment)
(Title or rank)"

Sec. 147.551. Jurat Form. Notwithstanding section 147.542 of the Revised Code, a jurat may take the following form:

"State of Ohio
County of.................

Sworn to or affirmed and subscribed before me by (signature of person making jurat) this date of (date).

(Signature of notary public administering jurat)
(Affix seal here)
(Title of rank)
(Commission expiration date)"

147.56 Notarial act performed prior to January 1, 1974.

A notarial act performed prior to January 1, 1974, is not affected by sections 147.51 to 147.58 of the Revised Code. These sections provide an additional method of proving notarial acts and do not diminish or invalidate the recognition accorded to notarial acts by other laws or regulations of this state.

Effective Date: 01-01-1974

147.57 Uniformity of the law.

Sections 147.51 to 147.58 of the Revised Code shall be so interpreted as to make uniform the laws of those states which enact it.

Effective Date: 01-01-1974

147.58 Uniform recognition of acknowledgments act.

Sections 147.51 to 147.58 of the Revised Code may be cited as the "Uniform Recognition of Acknowledgments Act."

Effective Date: 01-01-1974

Sec. 147.59. Designated Alternative Signer. (A) An individual whose physical characteristics limit the individual's ability to sign a document presented for notarization may direct a designated alternative signer to sign on the individual's behalf, if all of the following are met:

(1) The individual clearly indicates, through oral, verbal, physical, electronic, or mechanical means, to the notary public the individual's intent for the designated alternative signer to sign the individual's name on the notarial document.

(2) Both the individual and the designated alternative signer provide satisfactory identification to the notary public.

(3) The designated alternative signer signs the document in the presence of the notary public.

(4) The designated alternative signer is not named in the document.

(5) The notarial certificate provided to the individual gives the name of the designated alternative signer and states that the document was signed under this section at the direction of the individual.

(B) An individual may use a designated alternative signer to perform an online notarial act if all of the requirements of division (A) of this section are met.

Sec. 147.591. Electronic Documents. (A) As used in this section, "electronic document," "electronic seal," "electronic signature," and "online notarization" have the same meanings as in section 147.60 of the Revised Code.

(B) (1) An electronic document that is signed in the physical presence of the notary public with an electronic signature and notarized with an electronic seal shall be considered an original document.

(2) Notwithstanding any other provision of the Revised Code to the contrary, a printed copy of a document executed electronically by the parties and acknowledged or sworn before a notary acting pursuant to this section shall be accepted by county auditors, engineers, and recorders for purposes of approval, transfer, and recording to the same extent as any other document that is submitted by an electronic recording method and shall not be rejected solely by reason of containing electronic signatures or an electronic notarization, including an online notarization, if that document contains the certificate required under division (G) of section 147.542 of the Revised Code, including the notification required under division (G)(7) of that section.

(C) Any notary public may obtain an electronic seal and an electronic signature for the purposes of notarizing documents under this section.

(D) A notary public shall comply with the provisions of section 147.66 of the Revised Code pertaining to the electronic seal and electronic signature.

Sec. 147.60. Definitions. As used in this section and sections 147.61 to 147.66 of the Revised Code:

(A) "Appear in person" means being in the same physical location as another person and being close enough to hear, communicate with, and exchange tangible identification credentials with that individual. "Appear in person" also means being in a different location as another person and interacting with that individual by means of live two-way, audio-video communication.

(B) "Credential analysis" means a process or service operating according to standards adopted by the secretary of state under section 147.62 of the Revised Code through which a third person affirms the validity of a government-issued identification credential through review of public and proprietary data sources.

(C) "Electronic" means relating to technology having electrical, digital, magnetic, wireless, optical, electromagnetic, or similar capabilities.

(D) "Electronic document" means information that is created, generated, sent, communicated, received, or stored in an electronic medium and is retrievable in perceivable form.

(E) "Electronic seal" means information within a notarized electronic document to which all of the following apply:

(1) The information confirms the notary public's name, jurisdiction, and commission expiration date.

(2) The information generally corresponds to the contents, layout, and format of the notary public's seal for use on paper documents, as required under section 147.04 of the Revised Code.

(F) "Electronic signature" means an electronic sound, symbol, or process attached to or logically associated with an electronic document and executed or adopted by a natural person with the intent to sign the electronic document.

(G) "Identity proofing" means a process or service operating according to standards adopted by the secretary of state under section 147.62 of the Revised Code through which a third person affirms the identity of a natural person through the review of personal information from public and proprietary data sources.

(H) "Notarial act" means the performance of a function authorized under sections 147.07 and 147.51 of the Revised Code. "Notarial act" does not include the taking or certifying of depositions.

(I) "Online notarization" means a notarial act performed by means of live two-way video and audio conference technology that conforms to the standards adopted by the secretary of state under section 147.62 of the Revised Code.

(J) "Online notary public" means a notary public who has been duly appointed and commissioned under section 147.01 of the Revised Code and has received authorization by the secretary of state under section 147.63 of the Revised Code to perform online notarizations.

(K) "Principal" means a natural person whose electronic signature is notarized in an online notarization, or the natural person taking an oath or affirmation from the online notary public. "Principal" does not include a natural person taking an oath or giving an affirmation in the capacity of a witness for the online notarization.

(L) "Remote presentation" means transmission to an online notary public through live two- way video and audio conference technology of an image of a government-issued identification credential that is of sufficient quality to enable the online notary public to identify the principal seeking the online notary public's services and to perform credential analysis.

(M) "Territory of the United States" means the United States, Puerto Rico, the United States Virgin Islands, and any territory, insular possession, or other location subject to the jurisdiction of the United States.

Sec. 147.61. Applicability. Sections 147.60 to 147.66 of the Revised Code apply to online notarizations and online notaries public. To the extent that a provision of sections 147.60 to 147.66 of the Revised Code conflicts with another provision of this chapter or other applicable law, sections 147.60 to 147.66 of the Revised Code supersede the provision.

Sec. 147.62. Standards for Online Notarizations and Online Notaries Public. (A) The secretary of state shall adopt rules under Chapter 119. of the Revised Code necessary to implement, set, and maintain standards for online notarizations and online notaries public. Such rules shall address, at a minimum, all of the following:

(1) The standards, procedures, application forms, and fees for the authorization of a notary public to act as an online notary public;

(2) The means of performing online notarizations;

(3) Standards for the technology to be used in online notarizations;

(4) Standards for remote presentation, credential analysis, and identity proofing;

(5) Standards for the retention of records relating to online notarizations;

(6) The modification of forms of notarial certificates for any notarial act that is an online notarization;

(7) Standards and requirements for the termination of a notary public's authorization to perform online notarizations.

(B) The office of information technology in the department of administrative services shall provide assistance to the secretary of state relating to the equipment, security, and technological aspects of the standards established under this section.

Sec. 147.63. Application to be Authorized as Online Notary Public. (A) A notary public who has been duly appointed and commissioned under section 147.01 of the Revised Code, and who is a resident of this state, may apply to the secretary of state to be authorized to act as an online notary public during the term of that notary public's commission. A state resident commissioned as a notary public qualifies to be an online notary public by paying the fee described in section 147.631 of the Revised Code and submitting to the secretary of state an application in the form prescribed by the secretary that demonstrates to the satisfaction of the secretary that the applicant will comply with the standards adopted in rules under section 147.62 of the Revised Code and that the applicant is otherwise qualified to be an online notary.

(B)(1) Before an individual may be authorized to act as an online notary public, that individual shall successfully complete a course of instruction approved by the secretary of state and pass an examination based on the course. The content of the course shall include notarial rules, procedures, and ethical obligations pertaining to online notarization contained in sections 147.60 to 147.66 of the Revised Code or in any other law or rules of this state. The course may be taken in conjunction with the educational program required under section 147.021 of the Revised Code for a notary public commission.

(2) The secretary of state shall approve one business entity comprised of bar associations with statewide scope and regional presence that have expertise and experience in notary laws and processes to provide the course and administer the examination to become an online notary.

(C) The application required under division (A) of this section shall be transmitted electronically to the secretary of state and shall include all of the following information:

(1) The applicant's full legal name and official notary public name to be used in acting as an online notary public;

(2) A description of the technology the applicant intends to use in performing online notarizations;

(3) A certification that the applicant will comply with the rules adopted under section 147.62 of the Revised Code;

(4) An electronic mail address of the applicant;

(5) Any decrypting instructions, keys, codes, or software necessary to enable the application to be read;

(6) Proof of successful completion of the course and passage of the examination required under division (B) of this section;

(7) A disclosure of any and all license or commission revocations or other professional disciplinary actions taken against the applicant;

(8) Any other information that the secretary of state may require.

(D)(1) If the secretary of state is satisfied that an applicant meets the standards adopted in rules under section 147.62 of the Revised Code, and that the applicant is otherwise qualified to be an online notary public, then the secretary shall issue to the applicant a written authorization to perform online notarizations.

(2) Except as provided in division (D) (4) of this section, the authorization shall expire when the notary public's commission expires or is revoked under section 147.03, 147.031, or 147.032 of the Revised Code.

(3)(a) Except as provided in division (D) (5) of this section, the authorization shall be renewed when the notary public's commission is renewed.

(b) An authorization to perform online notarizations that is set to expire shall not be renewed unless the notary submits to the secretary of state through the entity authorized in this section all of the following:

(i) A fee, set by the secretary of state, of not more than four times the fee prescribed in division (B)(2) of section 147.031 of the Revised Code;

(ii) An application for renewal on a form prescribed by the secretary;

(iii) Evidence of having completed continuing education, as required under division (G) of this section.

(c) If a notary public's online notarization authorization expires before the notary submits the application for renewal, the secretary of state shall not renew that expired authorization but shall permit that person to apply for a new online notarization authorization.

(4) An authorization to perform online notarizations granted to an attorney admitted to the practice of law in this state by the Ohio supreme court shall expire on the earlier of five years after the date the authorization is granted or when the attorney's term of office as a notary public ends.

(5) An attorney authorized to perform online notarizations may apply to renew the attorney's authorization three months prior to the authorization's expiration date.

(4)(a) The secretary may deny an application for an online notary public if any of the required information is missing or incorrect on the application form.

(b) The secretary may also deny an application if the technology the applicant identifies pursuant to division (C)(2) of this section does not conform to the standards developed by the secretary pursuant to section 147.62 of the Revised Code.

(E) Nothing in this section shall be construed as prohibiting an online notary public from receiving, installing, and utilizing a software update to the technology that the online notary public disclosed pursuant to division (C)(2) of this section if that software update does not result in a technology that is materially different from the technology that the online notary public disclosed pursuant to division (C)(2) of this section.

(F)(1) If a notary public changes either the hardware or the software that the notary intends to use to carry out online notarizations, then the notary shall inform the secretary of this intent on a form prescribed by the secretary.

(2) If the secretary determines that the new hardware or software does not meet the standards prescribed in rules under section 147.62 of the Revised Code, then the secretary may suspend or revoke the notary's authority to perform online notarizations.

(G)(1) The secretary of state shall not renew an online notarization authorization unless the applicant has completed continuing education as required under rules adopted pursuant to division (G)(2) of this section.

(2) The secretary shall adopt rules in accordance with Chapter 119. of the Revised Code related to continuing education requirements for an online notarization authorization. The rules shall specify the number of hours of continuing education a notary must complete over the duration of the notary's license and may specify content to be included in the continuing education.

Sec. 147.631. Online Notary Fees. (A)(1) The secretary of state may charge a fee for the online notary course of instruction and examination to each person who is registering to be an online notary.

(2) The secretary shall not charge a fee to a notary obtaining an electronic seal and signature solely for the purpose of conducting notarizations as described in section 147.591 of the Revised Code.

(B) The notary public taking the online notary course of instruction and the examination shall remit the fee to the authorized entity that administered the online notary course of instruction and examination required by division (B) of section 147.63 of the Revised Code. The notary public shall remit to the secretary of state the portion of that fee specified pursuant to division (C)(2) of this section.

(C) The secretary of state shall adopt rules in accordance with Chapter 119. of the Revised Code to do both of the following:

(1) Establish the amount of the fee authorized by division (A) of this section, which shall not exceed four times the amount of the fee established pursuant to division (C)(1) of section 147.37 of the Revised Code;

(2) Establish the portion of the fee, not to exceed twenty dollars, that the notary public is required to remit to the secretary of state.

Sec. 147.64. Authority of Online Notary Public. (A)(1) Except as provided in division (A) (3) of this section, an online notary public has the authority to perform any notarial act as an online notarization.

(2) An electronic document notarized through an online notarization shall be considered an original document.

(3) An online notary public shall not take or certify a deposition as an online notarization.

(B) A notary public of this state who has been authorized by the secretary of state to perform online notarizations may perform online notarizations only if both of the following conditions are met:

(1) The online notary public is a resident of this state.

(2) The online notary public is located within the geographical boundaries of this state at the time of the online notarization.

(C)(1) A notary public may perform an online notarization by means of audio-video communication in compliance with this act and any other rules adopted by the secretary of state for any principal who is located within the territory of the United States.

(2) A notary public may perform an online notarization for a principal located outside the territory of the United States only if both of the following conditions are met:

(a) The act is not known by the notary public to be prohibited in the jurisdiction in which the principal is physically located at the time of the act.

(b) The record meets any of the following:

(i) Is part of, or pertains to, a matter that is to be filed with or is before a court, governmental entity, or other entity located in the territorial jurisdiction of the United States;

(ii) Involves real or personal property located in the territorial jurisdiction of the United States;

(ii) Is part of, or pertains to, a transaction substantially connected with the United States.

(D) If an online notarization requires a principal to appear before an online notary public, the principal shall appear in person before the notary public and the principal and the notary public shall each sign the record with an electronic signature.

(E)(1) In performing an online notarization, a notary public shall determine from personal knowledge or satisfactory evidence of identity as described in division (E)(2) of this section that the principal appearing before the notary by means of live audio-video communication is the individual that he or she purports to be.

(2) A notary public has satisfactory evidence of identity if the notary can identify the individual who appears in person before the notary by means of audio-video communication based on either of the following:

(a) All of the following:

(i) Remote presentation by the principal of a government- issued identification credential, including a passport or driver's license, that contains the signature and photograph of the principal;

(ii) Credential analysis of the identification credentials provided;

(iii) Identity proofing of the principal.

(b) Verification by one or more credible witnesses who appear in person before the notary and who can be identified by either personal knowledge or all of the following:

(i) Presentation of a government-issued identification credential, including a passport or driver's license, that contains the signature and photograph of the witness;

(ii) Credential analysis of the identification credentials provided;

(iii) Identity proofing of the witness.

(F) The secretary of state shall include in rules adopted under section 147.62 of the Revised Code modified forms of notarial certificates for any notarial act that is an online notarization.

Sec. 147.65. Electronic Journals. (A) An online notary public shall maintain one or more electronic journals in which the online notary public records, in chronological order, all online notarizations that the online notary public performs. The electronic journal shall enable access by a password or other secure means of authentication and be in a tamper-evident electronic format complying with the rules of the secretary of state adopted under section 147.62 of the Revised Code.

(B) For every online notarization, the online notary public shall record the following information in the electronic journal:

(1) The date and time of the notarial act;

(2) The type of notarial act;

(3) The title or a description of the record being notarized, if any;

(4) The electronic signature of each principal;

(5) The printed full name and address of each principal;

(6) If identification of the principal is based on personal knowledge, a statement to that effect;

(7) If identification of the principal is based on satisfactory evidence of identity pursuant to division (E)(2) of section 147.64 of the Revised Code, a description of the evidence relied upon, including the date of issuance or expiration of any identification credential presented;

(8) If identification of the principal is based on a credible witness or witnesses, the name of the witness or witnesses;

(9) If the notarization was not performed at the online notary public's business address, the address where the notarization was performed;

(10) A description of the online notarization system used;

(11) The fee, if any, charged by the notary;

(12) The name of the jurisdiction in which the principal was located at the time of the online notarization;

(13) The recording upon which the identification of the principal is based, as required under division (D)(3) of this section;

(14) Any other information required by the secretary of state.

(C) An online notary public shall not record a social security number in the electronic journal.

(D) An online notary public shall do all of the following:

(1) Take reasonable steps to ensure the integrity, security, and authenticity of online notarizations;

(2) Take reasonable steps to ensure that the two-way, audio-video communication used in an online notarization is secure from unauthorized interception;

(3) Create and maintain pursuant to this section a complete recording of the audio-video communication that is the basis for identification of a principal for each online notarization;

(4) Maintain a backup for the electronic journal required by division (A) of this section and the audio-video recordings required by division (D)(3) of this section;

(5)(a) Safeguard the electronic journal and all other notarial records by doing all of the following:

(i) Not allowing the electronic journal to be used by another notary;

(ii) Creating the audio-video recording required under division (D)(3) of this section in a tamper-evident electronic format complying with the rules of the secretary of state adopted under section 147.62 of the Revised Code;

(iii) Protecting the electronic journal and audio-video recordings from unauthorized use.

(b) An online notary public may use a third party to keep and store the electronic journal. The secretary of state shall adopt, in rules under Chapter 119. of the Revised Code, standards pertaining to the use of such a third party.

(6) Surrender or destroy the electronic journal and all other notarial records only by rule of law, by court order, or at the direction of the secretary of state;

(7) Not surrender the electronic journal to an employer upon termination of employment.

(E)(1) An employer shall not retain the electronic journal of an employee who is an online notary public when the notary's employment ceases.

(2) Notwithstanding division (E)(1) of this section, an online notary public may make an agreement with a current or former employer pursuant to division (D)(5)(b) of this section.

(3) An online notary public may use any current or former employer approved as a repository by the secretary of state to meet all applicable repository requirements of this section or section 147.66 of the Revised Code and any associated rules.

(F)(1) Except as provided in division (E) of section 147.66 of the Revised Code, an electronic journal required under division (A) of this section and the audio-video recordings required by division (D)(3) of this section shall be maintained by the online notary public during the term of the online notary public's authorization to perform online notarizations.

(2) Upon the expiration, pursuant to division (D) of section 147.63 of the Revised Code, of the notary public's authorization to conduct online notarizations, the online notary public shall transmit the electronic journal to the secretary of state or to a repository approved by the secretary of state. The secretary of state or repository shall maintain the electronic journal for a period of ten years. If the electronic journal is transmitted to a repository, the online notary public shall inform the secretary of state where the journal is located during this period.

(3) If the notary public renews the notary public's authorization to conduct online notarizations pursuant to division (D) of section 147.63 of the Revised Code, the notary public shall, beginning on the date the renewal is effective, maintain a new electronic journal in accordance with this section.

(G) (1) Except as provided in divisions (G)(2) and (3) of this section, any person may inspect or request a copy of an entry or entries in the online notary public's journal, provided that all of the following are met:

(a) The person specifies the month, year, type of record, and name of the principal for the notarial act, in a signed tangible or electronic request.

(b) The notary does not surrender possession or control of the journal.

(c) The person is shown or given a copy of only the entry or entries specified.

(d) A separate new entry is made in the journal, explaining the circumstances of the request and noting any related act of copy certification by the online notary public.

(2) Notwithstanding division (A)(5) of section 147.141 of the Revised Code, an online notary public may certify copies made from the online notary public's electronic journal.

(3) An online notary public who has a reasonable and explainable belief that a person requesting information from the notary's journal has a criminal or other inappropriate purpose may deny access to any entry or entries.

(4) An attorney authorized to conduct online notarizations shall only allow inspection, or provide copies, of an entry or entries in the attorney's journal if the requesting party was a principal in the transaction or transactions to which the journal entry or entries apply or if the requesting party is acting on a principal's behalf. An attorney may deny a request to inspect or receive copies of a journal entry based on attorney-client privilege.

(5) The secretary of state, or a repository approved by the secretary of state, shall only allow inspection, or provide copies of, an entry or entries in a journal deposited with the secretary or the repository by an attorney authorized to conduct online notarizations if the requesting party was a principal in the transaction or transactions to which the journal entry or entries apply or if the requesting party is acting on a principal's behalf.

(H)(1) The journal may be examined and copied without restriction by a law enforcement officer, as defined in section 2901.01 of the Revised Code, in the course of an official investigation, subpoenaed by court order, or surrendered at the direction of the secretary of state.

(2) Notwithstanding division (H)(1) of this section, an attorney authorized to conduct online notarizations may object to the examination, or copying, of the attorney's journal pursuant to division (H)(1) of this section based on attorney- client privilege.

Sec. 147.66. Steps to Ensure Security. (A) An online notary public shall take reasonable steps to ensure that any device or software used to create an official electronic signature is current and has not been recalled or declared vulnerable by the device or software's manufacturer, seller, or developer.

(B) (1) An online notary public shall do both of the following:

(a) Except as provided in division (D)(5)(b) of section 147.65 of the Revised Code, keep the online notary public's electronic journal, official electronic signature, and electronic seal secure and under the online notary public's exclusive control;

(b) Use the online notary public's official electronic signature and electronic seal only for performing online notarizations or notarizations pursuant to section 147.591 of the Revised Code.

(2) An online notary public shall not allow another person to use the online notary public's electronic journal, official electronic signature, or electronic seal.

(C)(1) A third party keeping and storing electronic journals for online notaries public pursuant to division (D)(5) (b) of section 147.65 of the Revised Code shall immediately, upon discovery, notify the secretary of state, an appropriate law enforcement agency, and any affected online notaries public of the unauthorized access, modification, transfer, duplication, or use of any electronic journals in the third party's possession or control.

(2) If notice has not already been given pursuant to division (C)(1) of this section, a third party keeping and storing electronic journals for online notaries public pursuant to division (D)(5)(b) of section 147.65 of the Revised Code shall immediately, upon discovery, notify the secretary of state and any affected online notaries public of the loss of any electronic journals in the third party's possession or control.

(3) If notice has not already been given pursuant to division (C)(1) or (2) of this section, an online notary public shall immediately, upon discovery, notify an appropriate law enforcement agency and the secretary of state of the unauthorized access, modification, transfer, duplication, or use of the online notary public's electronic journal, official electronic signature, or electronic seal.

(4) If notice has not already been given pursuant to division (C)(1), (2), or (3) of this section, an online notary public shall immediately notify the secretary of state of the loss of the online notary public's electronic journal, official electronic signature, or electronic seal.

(D) An online notary public shall attach the online notary public's electronic signature and electronic seal to the notarial certificate of an electronic document in a manner that is capable of independent verification and renders any subsequent change or modification to the electronic document evident.

(E)(1)(a) Upon resignation, revocation, or expiration without renewal of an online notary public commission, the online notary public shall transmit the electronic journal to the secretary of state or to a repository approved by the secretary of state. This requirement does not apply to electronic journals that, as of the date of the resignation or expiration, were no longer kept in accordance with division (F) of section 147.65 of the Revised Code. If the electronic journal is transmitted to a repository, the online notary public shall inform the secretary of state where the journal is located during this period.

(b) Upon death or adjudicated incompetence of a current or former notary public, the executor or administrator of the online notary public's estate, the notary's guardian, or any other person knowingly in possession of the online notary public's electronic journal, shall transmit the journal to the secretary of state or to a repository approved by the secretary of state.

(2) The online notary public, the notary's personal representative or guardian, or the administrator or the executor of the notary's estate shall provide access instructions to the secretary of state for any electronic journal maintained or stored by the online notary public, upon commission resignation, revocation, or expiration without renewal, or upon the death or adjudicated incompetence of the online notary public, if that person is in possession of such instructions.

(3) The secretary of state or repository receiving a journal transmitted under division (E) (1) of this section shall maintain the journal for a period of ten years.

147.99 Penalty.

(A) Whoever violates section 147.10 of the Revised Code shall be fined not more than five hundred dollars.

(B) Whoever violates section 147.14 of the Revised Code shall be fined not more than one hundred dollars or imprisoned not more than thirty days, or both.

Effective Date: 10-01-1953

147.371 Duplicate commission.

(A) Upon receipt of a fee of two dollars and an affidavit that the original commission of a notary public has been lost or destroyed, a duplicate commission as notary public shall be issued by the secretary of state.

(B) Upon receipt of a fee of two dollars and the properly completed, prescribed form for a name and address change under division (C) of section 147.05 of the Revised Code, the secretary of state shall issue a duplicate commission as a notary public.

Effective Date: 06-06-2001; 06-30-2005

NOTARY MODERNIZATION ACT

Ohio Administrative Rules
Effective Date: 9-22-2019
111: 6-1 Definitions.

(A) "Applicant" means any person applying for a notary commission pursuant to section 147.01 or an online notary authorization pursuant to section 147.63 of the Revised Code.

(B) "Authorized education and testing provider" and "authorized provider" mean those entities approved by the secretary of state to offer education and testing to notary commission applicants and attorneys pursuant to section 147.021 of the Revised Code and section 147.63 for online notary authorization.

(C) "Credential analysis" means the same as provided in division (B) of section 147.60 of the Revised Code.

(D) "Disqualifying offense" means the same as division (C) of section 147.011 of the Revised Code.

(E) "Dynamic knowledge-based authentication" means a form of identity proofing as defined by division (G) of section 147.60 of the Revised Code that is based on a set of questions formulated from public or private data sources for which the principal has not provided a prior answer.

(F) "Document" means a record consisting of information inscribed on a tangible medium or that is created, generated, sent, communicated, received, or stored in an electronic medium and is retrievable in perceivable form. The term includes "electronic document."

(G) "Electronic document" means the same as provided in division (D) of section 147.60 of the Revised Code.

(H) "Electronic journal" means the chronological record of notarizations maintained by a notary public in an electronic format and described in section 147.65 of the Revised Code.

(I) "Electronic notarial act" means a notarial act defined in section 147.51 of the Revised Code that is performed using an official electronic signature and seal on an electronic document, by an individual commissioned as a notary public pursuant to section 147.01 of the Revised Code.

(J) "Electronic Seal" means the same as provided in division (E) of section 147.60 of the Revised Code.

(K) "Electronic Signature" means the same as provided in division (F) of section 147.60 of the Revised Code.

(L) "Exclusive control" means accessible by and attributable solely to the notary public to the exclusion of all other persons and entities, either through being in the direct physical custody of the notary public or through being secured with one or more biometric password, token or other authentication technologies.

(M) "Notarial Act" for purposes of this chapter means an official act that a notary public is authorized to perform by law and as provided in section 147.60(H) of the Revised Code.

(N) "Notarial Certificate" means the portion of a notarized document that is completed by a notary public and that bears the notary public's signature, seal and language as required by law.

(O) "Notary commission" is a commission issued to a notary public pursuant to sections 147.01 – 147.13 of the Revised Code.

(P) "Notary Public" means an individual commissioned by the secretary of state under section 147.01 of the Revised Code. A notary public does not have the authority to perform online notarizations unless also authorized by the secretary of state to perform an online notarization, however, a notary public may engage in an electronic notarial act as permitted under section 147.591 of the Revised Code.

(Q) "Official electronic signature" means the electronic signature used by a notary public commissioned pursuant to section 147.01 of the Revised Code; and the electronic signature used by a notary public who is authorized as an online notary public pursuant to section 147.63 of the Revised Code.

(R) "Online notarization" means the same as provided in section 147.60(I) of Revised Code. The term includes "online notarial act."

(S) "Online notarization system" means a set of applications, programs, hardware, software, or technology designed to enable a notary public to perform online notarial acts.

(T) "Online Notary Public" means the same as division (J) of section 147.60 of the Revised Code.

(U) "Principal" means a person whose signature is notarized or a person, other than a credible witness, taking an oath or affirmation from the notary.

(V) "Real time" means the actual span of uninterrupted, simultaneous communication during which all parts of an online notarial act using audio-video communication occur.

(W) "Record" includes a document as defined in this chapter; an entry in a journal maintained by an online notary public pursuant to section 147.65 of the Revised Code; the audio-video recording required in section 147.65(D)(3) of the Revised Code; and a notary public's record kept by the secretary of state under section 147.05 of the revised code.

(X) "Remote presentation" means the same as provided in division (L) of section 147.60 of the Revised Code.

Promulgated Under: 119.03

Statutory Authority: 147.021, 147.031, 147.032, 147.08, 147.37, 147.62, 147.63, 147.65

Rule Amplifies: 147.021, 147.031, 147.032, 147.08, 147.37, 147.62, 147.63, 147.64, 147.65

111: 6-2 Notary Commission Education and Testing Requirements.

(A) An authorized education and testing provider, as described in sections 147.21 and 147.63 of the Revised Code, must be approved by the secretary of state. A potential authorized education and testing provider must submit a request to be approved as an authorized provider to the secretary of state and must respond to the secretary of state's request for information.

(B) The secretary of state shall provide information on its official website to inform applicants of the authorized providers' names and contact information.

(C) Curriculum for notary commission education shall include, but is not limited to, all of the following:

(1) The terms of a notary commission;

(2) Requirements to update and renew a commission;

(3) Reporting requirement if a notary public is convicted or pleads guilty or no contest to a disqualifying offense;

(4) Geographic jurisdiction of a notary public;

(5) Maintaining a notarial journal;

(6) Requirements for a notary seal;

(7) What constitutes a notarial act that complies with applicable Ohio law and administrative rules;

(8) How to perform a compliant notarial act, including examples involving commonly notarized documents;

(9) Administration of an oath or affirmation;

(10) Verifying the identity of the principal;

(11) The taking of an acknowledgment;

(12) The administration of a jurat;

(13) The manner of taking depositions;

(14) Signatures by mark;

(15) Method to notarize a document signed by a designated alternative signer;

(16) Overview and examples of prohibited acts;

(17) Explanation of electronic notarizations;

(18) What constitutes unauthorized immigration consultant acts and the unauthorized practice of law by a notary;

(19) The fees a notary public is permitted to charge;

(20) Mandatory reporting that is required of a notary;

(21) The conditions under which a commission may be revoked; and

(22) Investigation and disciplinary processes.

(D) Curriculum for online notary authorizations education shall include but not be limited to all notarial rules, procedures and ethical obligations pertaining to online notarizations under sections 147.60 to 147.66 of the Revised Code.

(E) Curriculum for continuing education for commissions and online authorizations shall include, but not be limited to, any updates to Ohio notary law or the administrative rules.

(F) Applicants for a notary commission who are required to successfully pass a test pursuant to sections 147.021 and 147.63 of the Revised Code must be tested on all of topics listed in division (C) and (D) of this rule. An authorized education and testing provider must offer multiple curriculum tests so that there is not one uniform test in circulation.

(G) An authorized education and testing provider must seek approval from the secretary of state prior to providing education and testing services to applicants. The secretary of state may request documentation to ensure the authorized provider has met the standards. An authorized provider must notify the secretary of state of material modifications to its educational program and testing at least ten days prior to such modifications, and implement such modifications only upon receiving the approval of the secretary of state.

(H) An authorized provider must electronically share data related to an applicant's education completion and testing results with the secretary of state, upon request of the secretary of state.

Promulgated Under: 119.03

Statutory Authority: 147.021

Rule Amplifies: 147.01, 147.021, 147.63

111: 6-3 Fee for Application, Education and Testing.

(A) Non-Attorney Notary Commission Application, Education and Testing Requirements.

(1) Non-attorney notary commission applicants must complete a three-hour education program and pass a test administered by an authorized provider.

(2) The applicant shall submit to the authorized provider a fee of one hundred thirty dollars for the required education and testing as described in (A)(1) of this rule.

(3) An applicant who fails the test required by section 147.021 of the Revised Code, may apply to retake the exam not sooner than 30 days following the date of his or her last examination, and no later than 6 months following the issuance of the criminal records check. Should an applicant fail the exam a second time, the applicant must

re-start the process with a new application including the fee as described in (A)(2) of this rule.

(4) An applicant must pay a fee of fifteen dollars to the secretary of state upon filing the application for a commission.

(B) Attorney Notary Commission Application and Education Requirements.

(1) Attorney notary commission applicants must successfully complete a three-hour education program conducted by an authorized provider.

(2) The applicant shall submit to the authorized provider a fee of seventy-five dollars for the required education described in (B)(1) of this rule.

(3) An applicant must pay a fee of fifteen dollars to the secretary of state upon filing the application for a commission.

(C) Notary Commission Renewal Application and Education Requirements

(1) A non-attorney notary commission renewal applicant must successfully complete a one-hour education program, no earlier than twelve (12) months prior to the expiration of their commission, conducted by an authorized provider.

(2) The applicant shall submit to the authorized provider a fee of forty-five dollars for the required education described in (C)(1) of this rule.

(3) An applicant must pay a fee of fifteen dollars to the secretary of state upon filing the application for a commission.

(D) Online Notarization Authorization Application, Education and Testing Requirements

(1) A notary public who has been duly appointed and commissioned under section 147.01 of the Revised Code, and who is a resident of this state, may apply to the secretary of state for authorization to perform online notarizations public during the term of that notary public's commission.

(2) The applicant must successfully complete a two-hour education program and pass a test administered by an authorized provider.

(3) The applicant shall submit to the authorized education and testing provider a fee of two hundred fifty dollars for the required education and testing program.

(4) Should an applicant fail the test required by section 147.63 of the Revised Code, the applicant may apply to retake the exam not sooner than 30 days following the date of the applicant's most recent examination, and no later than 6 months following date of completion of the education program. Should the applicant fail the exam a second time, the applicant must re-start the process with a new application including the fee described in (D)(3) of this rule.

(4) An applicant must pay a fee of twenty dollars to the secretary of state upon filing the application for authorization to perform online notarizations.

(E) Online Notarization Authorization Renewal Application and Education Requirements

(1) A non-attorney notary public authorized to perform online notarial acts may apply to renew the authorization to perform online notarizations no earlier than three months prior to expiration of the applicant's notary commission.

(2) An attorney notary public authorized to perform online notarial acts may apply to renew the authorization to perform online notarizations no earlier than three months prior to expiration of the online notary authorization.

(3) An applicant must successfully complete a one-hour education program, no earlier than twelve (12) months prior to the expiration of their commission, conducted by an authorized provider.

(4) The applicant shall submit a fee to an authorized provider of one hundred sixty dollars for the required continuing education described in division (E)(3) of this rule.

(5) An applicant must pay a fee of twenty dollars to the secretary of state upon filing the application for a commission.

Promulgated Under: 119.03

Statutory Authority: 147.37, 147.62, 147.63

Rule Amplifies: 147.021, 147.63

111: 6-4 Electronic Notarial Certificate Forms

For electronic notarial acts performed by a notary public for a principal in the notary public's physical presence; and for electronic notarial acts performed by an online notary public using audio-video communication for a principal not in the online notary public's physical presence; the notarial certificate forms provided in section 147.55 of the Revised Code may be used and are sufficient for their respective purposes under any section of the Revised Code, if the forms include these or similar statements, as applicable:

(a) "This certificate pertains to an electronic notarial act performed with the principal(s) in my physical presence"; or

(b) "This certificate pertains to an electronic notarial act performed with the principal(s) appearing online using audio-video communication."

Promulgated Under: 119.03

Statutory Authority: 147.62, 147.64

Rule Amplifies: 147.591, 147.60, 147.66

111: 6-5 Requirements for Online Notarial Acts.

(A) An online notary public must be physically located within the boundaries of Ohio at the time the notarial act takes place; however, the signer may be located anywhere within the territory of the United States or outside the United States only if the conditions set forth in section 147.64(C)(2) are met.

(B) Online notarizations must occur with the use of an online notarization system, which has two-way live audio and video conference technology, and that meets the following requirements:

(1) The online notary public must be able to verify the identity of the remotely located individual at the time the signature is taken by one of the following methods:

(a) The online notary public's personal knowledge of the individual;

(b) Each of the following:

(i) Remote presentation of an unexpired government-issued identification credential that contains the photograph and signature of the individual to the online notary public by means of communication technology;

(ii) Credential analysis of the identification credential in accordance with section (B)(4) of this rule; and

(iii) Identity proofing of the individual in accordance with section (B)(5) of this rule.

(c) Oath or affirmation of a single credible witness who personally knows the individual and either is personally known to the online notary public or who is identified by the online notary public under paragraph (b) of this subsection.

(2) A credible witness under subsection (B)(1)(c) may appear before the online notary public by means of communication technology that complies with Chapter 147 of the Ohio Revised Code and these rules.

(3) Credential analysis and identity proofing must be performed by a reputable third person who has provided reasonable evidence to the online notary public of the person's ability to satisfy the requirements of Chapter 147 of the Ohio Revised Code and this rule.

(4) Credential analysis must utilize public or private data sources to confirm the validity of an identification credential and must, at a minimum:

(a) use automated software processes to aid the online notary public in verifying the identity of a remotely located individual;

(b) ensure that the identification credential passes an authenticity test, consistent with sound commercial practices that:

(i) use appropriate technologies to confirm the integrity of visual, physical, or cryptographic security features;

(ii) use appropriate technologies to confirm that the identification credential is not fraudulent or inappropriately modified;

(iii) use information held or published by the issuing source or an authoritative source, as available, to confirm the validity of identification credential details; and

(iv) provide output of the authenticity test to the online notary public;

(c) enable the online notary public to visually compare for consistency:

(i) the information and photograph on the presented credential, and

(ii) the remotely located individual as viewed by the online notary public in real time through communication technology;

(d) require a government-issued identification credential that:

(i) is an unexpired government-issued identification credential that contains the photograph and signature of the individual; and

(ii) may be imaged, photographed, and video recorded under applicable state and federal law; and

(iii) can be subjected to credential analysis.

(e) include an image capture procedure that confirms that:

(i) the remotely located individual is in possession of the credential at the time of the notarial act;

(ii) credential images submitted for credential analysis have not been manipulated; and

(iii) credential images match the credential in the possession of the remotely located individual; and

(f) require the captured image of the identification credential to:

(i) be of sufficient image resolution to perform credential analysis in accordance with the requirements of this subsection;

(ii) be of sufficient image resolution to enable visual inspection of the credential by the notary public; and

(iii) include all images necessary to perform visual inspection and credential analysis in accordance with the requirements of this subsection, including the identity page of any passport and the front and back images of any identification card.

(5) Identity proofing shall be performed by means of a knowledge-based authentication that meets the following requirements:

(a) each remotely located individual must answer a quiz consisting of a minimum of five questions related to the remotely located individual's personal history or identity, formulated from public or private data sources;

(b) each question must have a minimum of five possible answer choices;

(c) at least 80% of the questions must be answered correctly;

(d) all questions must be answered within two minutes;

(e) if the remotely located individual fails the first attempt, the individual may retake the quiz two times within 48 hours;

(f) during a retake of the quiz, a minimum of 40% of the prior questions must be replaced;

(g) if the remotely located individual fails the second attempt, the individual is not permitted to retry with the same notary or the same third person providing the identity proofing service within 24 hours of the second failed attempt; and

(h) the online notary public must not be able to see or record the questions or answers.

(6) The online notarization system used must meet the following criteria:

(a) The persons communicating must simultaneously see and speak to one another.

(b) The signal transmission must be live, real time.

(c) The signal transmission must be secure from interception or access by anyone other than the persons communicating.

(d) The technology must provide sufficient audio clarity and video resolution to enable the notary to communicate with the signer and utilize the permissible signer identification methods.

(e) The system must provide confirmation that the electronic document presented is the same as the electronic document notarized.

(f) Allow for the affixation of the notarial certificate, signature and seal.

(g) Allow for viewing the notarial certificate, signature and seal.

(h) Provide a method for determining if the electronic document has been altered after the electronic notarial seal has been affixed and the electronic notarial act has been completed.

(i) Provide a method of generating a paper copy of the document including the notarial certificate, signature and seal and any other document associated with the execution of the notarial act.

(C) If the signer or online notary public must exit the audio-video communication session, the audio-video communication link is broken, or the resolution or quality of the transmission becomes such that the electronic notary public believes the process has been compromised and cannot be completed, the identity authentication process and any incomplete online notarial acts must be started from the beginning.

(D) The online notary public shall refuse to perform an online notarization if:

(1) the online notary public is unable to verify the identity of the principal;

(2) the online notary public is unable to verify the security of the two way audio visual transmission;

(3) the signature of the principal cannot be attached to the electronic document; or

(4) the online notarization system or technology cannot render the notarial act tamper-evident.

Promulgated Under: 119.03

Statutory Authority: 147.62

Rule Amplifies: 147.62, 147.64, 147.65

111: 6-6 Complaints.

Any person may submit a complaint in writing to the secretary of state and allege that a notary public has violated one or more of the provisions of Chapter 147 of the Revised Code. The complaint must include:

(a) the name of the notary public;

(b) the notary public's commission number, if known,;

(c) an explanation of the reason for the complaint and, if known, the citation of each statutory provision which the notary public is alleged to have violated;

(d) a copy of each document related to the matter; and

(e) the name, phone number, address, email address and signature of the person submitting the complaint.

Promulgated Under: 119.03

Statutory Authority: 147.032

Rule Amplifies: 147.032

111: 6-7 Investigations and Discipline.

(A) Upon receiving a signed complaint, or if the secretary of state has a reasonable basis to believe that a violation of Chapter 147 of the Ohio Revised Code has occurred, then the secretary of state shall designate an authorized agent to investigate the violation.

(B) After an investigation, the authorized agent shall forward the agent's findings to the secretary of state, the person who filed the complaint and the notary public named in the complaint (the "respondent"). If, upon reviewing the agent's findings, the secretary of state determines a violation of Chapter 147 of the Ohio Revised Code may have, or may occur, and wants to take action with respect to such possible violation, it shall send a written notice of such determination to the person who filed the complaint and the respondent. The respondent shall have fourteen (14) days to request a hearing from the secretary of state. The request must be sent to the secretary of state with a copy to the director of business services of the secretary of state. The secretary of state shall schedule the hearing within fifteen (15) days after receiving the request for a hearing and shall promptly notify the respondent of such date. Once a hearing is scheduled, the secretary of state shall appoint a hearing officer. The hearing officer must be admitted to the practice of law in Ohio and be knowledgeable of Ohio notary laws. The hearing date may be continued by the hearing officer, at the request of the secretary of state or the request of the respondent. The hearing shall be conducted in accordance with Chapter 119 of the Revised Code.

(C) Prior to the hearing, the respondent shall have the opportunity to answer the complaint by filing a written answer with the secretary of state. Any subpoenas for the hearing shall be requested from the hearing officer for issuance by the secretary of state. The hearing officer may receive evidence from the secretary of state and the respondent. The respondent may be represented by counsel; however, counsel is not required. A stenographic transcript of the oral testimony at the hearing shall be made.

(D) Following the hearing, the hearing officer shall issue a report and recommendation to the secretary of state within fourteen (14) days after completion of the hearing. A copy of this written report shall, at the time it is submitted to the secretary of state, be forwarded by electronic means and certified mail to the respondent or his or her counsel. If a violation of Chapter 147 of the Revised Code is found, the hearing officer may recommend the following:

(1) no action be taken;

(2) revoke the notary public's commission;

(3) suspend the notary public's commission for a specified period of time or until fulfillment of a condition, such as retraining, or both; or

(4) issue a letter of admonition to the notary public that shall be placed in the notary public's record.

(E) The respondent may file with the secretary of state written objections to the hearing officer's report within ten days of the date of the respondent's receipt of the report. The secretary of state shall render a decision within twenty (20) days after the receipt of the hearing officer's recommendation. The secretary of state shall send such decision to the respondent or his or her counsel by certified mail.

(F) If a hearing is not timely requested by the respondent, the secretary of state may take the following action:

(1) revoke the notary public's commission;

(2) suspend the notary public's commission for a specified period of time or until fulfillment of a condition, such as retraining, or both; or

(3) issue a letter of admonition to the notary public that shall be placed in the notary public's record.

(G) The respondent may appeal an adverse decision of the secretary of state under section 119.12 of the Revised Code.

Promulgated Under: 119.03

Statutory Authority: 147.032

Rule Amplifies: 147.032

Chapter 317
RECORDER

317.113 Certified complete English translation to accompany instrument.

The county recorder shall not accept for recording a deed or other instrument in writing that is executed or certified in whole or in part in a language other than the English language unless it complies with the requirements of sections 317.11, 317.111, and 317.112 of the Revised Code and is accompanied by a complete English translation certified as provided in this section. The translator of the deed or other instrument in writing shall certify that the translation is accurate and that the translator is competent to perform the translation. The translator shall sign and acknowledge the translation of the deed or other instrument in writing before a judge of a court of record in this state, a clerk of a court of record in this state, a county auditor, a county engineer, or a notary public.

A certificate of the translator that is substantially in the following form satisfies the requirements of this section:

"CERTIFICATE OF
TRANSLATOR

The undersigned, _____, hereby certifies that the document attached to
this certificate and made a part of this certificate has been translated into English by the undersigned; that the translation is accurate; and that the undersigned is competent to perform the translation.

_____
(Signature of Translator)
SSN: _____

State of _____
County of _____

The foregoing certificate of translator has been acknowledged before me this _____ day of _____, _____.

_____
(Signature of Judge or Officer Taking the Acknowledgment)"

This section does not apply to a deed or other instrument in writing executed or certified prior to August 20, 1996.

Effective Date: 02-01-2002

317.114 Standard format of instruments to be recorded.

(A) Except as otherwise provided in divisions (B) and (C) of this section, an instrument or document presented for recording to the county recorder shall have been prepared in accordance with all of the following requirements:

(1) Legible print size not smaller than a font size of ten;

(2) Minimum paper size of eight and one-half inches by eleven inches;

(3) Maximum paper size of eight and one-half inches by fourteen inches;

(4) Black or blue ink only;

(5) No use of highlighting;

(6) Margins of one-inch width on each side of each page of the instrument or document;

(7) A margin of one-inch width across the bottom of each page of the instrument or document;

(8) A three-inch margin of blank space across the top of the first page of each instrument or document to accommodate any certification or indorsement of the county engineer, county auditor, or county recorder, as may be required by law, with the right half of that margin being reserved for the indorsement of the county recorder required by section 317.12 of the Revised Code; and

(9) A one and one-half-inch margin of blank space across the top of each of the remaining pages of the instrument or document to accommodate any certification or indorsement of the county engineer, county auditor, or county recorder, as may be required by law.

(B)(1) Except as otherwise provided in division (B)(2) of this section, the county recorder shall accept for recording an instrument or document that does not conform to the requirements set forth in division (A) of this section but shall charge and collect the following additional fees for each such instrument or document: an additional base fee for the recorder's services of ten dollars and a housing trust fund fee of ten dollars, which shall be collected pursuant to section 317.36 of the Revised Code.

(2) The county recorder shall accept for recording an instrument or document that does not conform to the requirements set forth in division (A) of this section but shall not charge and collect the additional fees specified in division (B)(1) of this section for page numbers, hand-written, typed, or printed initials, bar codes, copyright information, trailing portions of signatures, plat description of any oil and gas well location or drilling unit or lease, or any other incidental information that is not essential to the recording process or to the legal validity of the instrument or document and that may appear in either of the side margins or in the bottom margin. In addition, notary stamps and seals and any signatures and initials that may appear within the instrument or document need not satisfy the font size requirement and no additional fees may be charged or collected by the county recorder for such a nonconformance.

(C) This section does not apply to any of the following:

(1) Any document that originates with any court or taxing authority;

(2) Any document authorized to be recorded under section 317.24 of the Revised Code;

(3) Any plat, as defined in section 711.001 of the Revised Code, that is required or authorized by the Revised Code to be recorded;

(4) Any document authorized to be recorded that originates from any state or federal agency;

(5) Any document executed before July 1, 2009.

Amended by 128th General Assembly File No. 17, SB 124, § 1, eff. 12/28/2009.

Effective Date: 2008 HB525 07-01-2009

Chapter 1337
POWER OF ATTORNEY

1337.12 Formality of execution.

(A)(1) An adult who is of sound mind voluntarily may create a valid durable power of attorney for health care by executing a durable power of attorney, in accordance with division (B) of section 1337.09 of the Revised Code, that authorizes an attorney in fact as described in division (A)(2) of this section to make health care decisions for the principal at any time that the attending physician of the principal determines that the principal has lost the capacity to make informed health care decisions for the principal. Except as otherwise provided in divisions (B) to (F) of section 1337.13 of the Revised Code, the authorization may include the right to give informed consent, to refuse to give informed consent, or to withdraw informed consent to any health care that is being or could be provided to the principal. Additionally, to be valid, a durable power of attorney for health care shall satisfy both of the following:

(a) It shall be signed at the end of the instrument by the principal and shall state the date of its execution.

(b) It shall be witnessed in accordance with division (B) of this section or be acknowledged by the principal in accordance with division (C) of this section.

(2) Except as otherwise provided in this division, a durable power of attorney for health care may designate any competent adult as the attorney in fact. The attending physician of the principal and an administrator of any nursing home in which the principal is receiving care shall not be designated as an attorney in fact in, or act as an attorney in fact pursuant to, a durable power of attorney for health care. An employee or agent of the attending physician of the principal and an employee or agent of any health care facility in which the principal is being treated shall not be designated as an attorney in fact in, or act as an attorney in fact pursuant to, a durable power of attorney for health care, except that these limitations do not preclude a principal from designating either type of employee or agent as the principal's attorney in fact if the individual is a competent adult and related to the principal by blood, marriage, or adoption, or if the individual is a competent adult and the principal and the individual are members of the same religious order.

(3) A durable power of attorney for health care shall not expire, unless the principal specifies an expiration date in the instrument. However, when a durable power of attorney contains an expiration date, if the principal lacks the capacity to make informed health care decisions for the principal on the expiration date, the instrument shall continue in effect until the principal regains the capacity to make informed health care decisions for the principal.

(B) If witnessed for purposes of division (A)(1)(b) of this section, a durable power of attorney for health care shall be witnessed by at least two individuals who are adults and who are not ineligible to be witnesses under this division. Any person who is related to the principal by blood, marriage, or adoption, any person who is designated as the attorney in fact in the instrument, the attending physician of the principal, and the administrator of any nursing home in which the principal is receiving care are ineligible to be witnesses.

The witnessing of a durable power of attorney for health care shall involve the principal signing, or acknowledging the principal's signature, at the end of the instrument in the presence of each witness. Then, each witness shall subscribe the witness's signature after the signature of the principal and, by doing so, attest to the witness's belief that the principal appears to be of sound mind and not under or subject to duress, fraud, or undue influence. The signatures of the principal and the witnesses under this division are not required to appear on the same page of the instrument.

(C) If acknowledged for purposes of division (A)(1)(b) of this section, a durable power of attorney for health care shall be acknowledged before a notary public, who shall make the certification described in section 147.53 of the Revised Code and also shall attest that the principal appears to be of sound mind and not under or subject to duress, fraud, or undue influence.

(D)(1) If a principal has both a valid durable power of attorney for health care and a valid declaration, division (B) of section 2133.03 of the Revised Code applies. If a principal has both a valid durable power of attorney for health care and a DNR identification that is based upon a valid declaration and if the declaration supersedes the durable power of attorney for health care under division (B) of section 2133.03 of the Revised Code, the DNR identification supersedes the durable power of attorney for health care to the extent of any conflict between the two. A valid durable power of attorney for health care supersedes any DNR identification that is based upon a do-not-resuscitate order that a physician issued for the principal which is inconsistent with the durable power of attorney for health care or a valid decision by the attorney in fact under a durable power of attorney.

(2) As used in division (D) of this section:

(a) "Declaration" has the same meaning as in section 2133.01 of the Revised Code.

(b) "Do-not-resuscitate order" and "DNR identification" have the same meanings as in section 2133.21 of the Revised Code.

Effective Date: 03-15-2001

Chapter 2319
AFFIDAVITS; DEPOSITIONS

2319.27 Fees for taking depositions - lien.

Except as section 147.08 of the Revised Code governs the fees chargeable by a notary public for services rendered in connection with depositions, the fees and expenses chargeable for the taking and certifying of a deposition by a person who is authorized to do so in this state, including, but not limited to, a shorthand reporter, stenographer, or person described in Civil Rule 28, may be established by that person subject to the qualification specified in this section, and may be different than the fees and expenses charged for the taking and certifying of depositions by similar persons in other areas of this state. Unless, prior to the taking and certifying of a deposition, the parties who request it agree that the fees or expenses to be charged may exceed the usual and customary fees or expenses charged in the particular community for similar services, such a person shall not charge fees or expenses in connection with the taking and certifying of the deposition that exceed those usual and customary fees and expenses.

The person taking and certifying a deposition may retain the deposition until the fees and expenses that he charged are paid. He also shall tax the costs, if any, of a sheriff or other officer who serves any process in connection with the taking of a deposition and the fees of the witnesses, and, if directed by a person entitled to those costs or fees, may retain the deposition until those costs or fees are paid.

Effective Date: 03-17-1987

Chapter 5301
CONVEYANCES; ENCUMBRANCES

5301.01 Acknowledgment of deed, mortgage, land contract, lease or memorandum of trust.

(A) A deed, mortgage, land contract as referred to in division (A)(2)

(b) of section 317.08 of the Revised Code, or lease of any interest in real property and a memorandum of trust as described in division (A) of section 5301.255 of the Revised Code shall be signed by the grantor, mortgagor, vendor, or lessor in the case of a deed, mortgage, land contract, or lease or shall be signed by the trustee in the case of a memorandum of trust. The signing shall be acknowledged by the grantor, mortgagor, vendor, or lessor, or by the trustee, before a judge or clerk of a court of record in this state, or a county auditor, county engineer, notary public, or mayor, who shall certify the acknowledgement and subscribe the official's name to the certificate of the acknowledgement.

(B)(1) If a deed, mortgage, land contract as referred to in division (A)

(2)(b) of section 317.08 of the Revised Code, lease of any interest in real property, or a memorandum of trust as described in division (A) of section 5301.255 of the Revised Code was executed prior to February 1, 2002, and was not acknowledged in the presence of, or was not attested by, two witnesses as required by this section prior to that date, both of the following apply:

(a) The instrument is deemed properly executed and is presumed to be valid unless the signature of the grantor, mortgagor, vendor, or lessor in the case of a deed, mortgage, land contract, or lease or of the settlor and trustee in the case of a memorandum of trust was obtained by fraud.

(b) The recording of the instrument in the office of the county recorder of the county in which the subject property is situated is constructive notice of the instrument to all persons, including without limitation, a subsequent purchaser in good faith or any other subsequent holder of an interest in the property, regardless of whether the instrument was recorded prior to, on, or after February 1, 2002.

(2) Division (B)(1) of this section does not affect any accrued substantive rights or vested rights that came into existence prior to February 1, 2002.

Effective Date: 07-20-2004; 2007 SB134 01-17-2008

OHIO RULES OF EVIDENCE
ARTICLE IX AUTHENTICATION AND IDENTIFICATION
EVID R 902.

SELF-AUTHENTICATION

Extrinsic evidence of authenticity as a condition precedent to admissibility is not required with respect to the following:

(1) Domestic public documents under seal.

A document bearing a seal purporting to be that of the United States, or of any State, district, Commonwealth, territory, or insular possession thereof, or the Panama Canal Zone, or the Trust Territory of the Pacific Islands, or of a political subdivision, department, officer, or agency thereof, and a signature purporting to be an attestation or execution.

***

(8) Acknowledged documents

Documents accompanied by a certificate of acknowledgment executed in the manner provided by law by a notary public or other officer authorized by law to take acknowledgments.

[Adopted eff. 7-1-80; amended eff. 7-1-07]

About the NNA

Since 1957, the National Notary Association has been committed to serving and educating the nation's Notaries. During that time, the NNA® has become known as the most trusted source of information for and about Notaries and Notary laws, rules and best practices.

The NNA serves Notaries through its NationalNotary.org website, social media, publications, annual conferences, seminars, online training and the NNA® Hotline, which offers immediate answers to specific questions about notarization.

In addition, the NNA offers the highest quality professional supplies, including official seals and stamps, recordkeeping journals, Notary certificates and Notary bonds.

Though dedicated primarily to educating and assisting Notaries, the NNA supports implementing effective Notary laws and informing the public about the Notary's vital role in today's society.

To learn more about the National Notary Association, visit NationalNotary.org. ■

Index

A

Acknowledgments.................... 25–29
Address change............................ 7
Advice...................................... 19
Affidavits............................... 30–32
Affirmations........................... 29–30
Apostilles................................ 19
Application for appointment 2–4
Appointment, Notary.................. 2–7
Authentication........................ 18–19
Authorized acts....................... 23–24
Awareness................................. 8–9

B

Blank documents......................... 16
Bond, Notary............................ 5–6

C

Certificate, Notary.................. 40–44
Certified copy............................. 24
Civil lawsuit............................... 50
Commission recorded by Secretary
 of State................................... 6
Credible identifying witness 10–11
Criminal records check................. 4

D

Death of Notary........................... 7

E

Depositions............................ 30–32
Designated alternative signer.. 13–14
Disqualifying interest 17
Durable power of attorney for
 health care............................. 21

E

Education and exam
 requirements........................... 4
Electronic journals................. 60–61
Electronic notarization rules........ 51
Electronic Notary certificate
 forms..................................... 52
Electronic seals and signatures..... 52
Errors and omissions insurance 6

F

Faxes..................................... 16–17
Fees...................................... 33–34
Fines..................................... 47–50
Foreign languages....................... 22

I

Identification documents (ID
 cards)................................ 11–12
Identifying document signers 9
Immigration........................... 19–20
Incomplete documents................ 16

Index | 105

J

Journal of notarial acts 35–39
Jurats.. 32–33
Jurisdiction 6

L

Laws pertaining to Notaries
   Public.. 63–103

M

Minors, notarizing for 14–15
Misconduct..47–50

N

Name change...7
National Notary Association........ 104

O

Oaths...29–30
Online notarization certificate
   forms 59–60
Online notarization fees 62
Online notarization rules and
   procedures.................................... 53–54
Online Notary Public
   renewal...54–55

P

Penalties..47–50
Personal appearance............................8
Personal knowledge of
   identity...9–10
Photocopies 16–17
Prohibited acts...............................47–50

R

Reasonable care...................................... 18
Refusal of service................................... 15
Renewing a Notary Public
   commission 5
Resignation of appointment.............7

S

Seal, Notary... 44–46
Signature by mark..........................12–13
Statement of particulars 40

T

Technology requirements for
   online notarial acts.................. 55–59
Term of office 6–7
Testimonium clause.................... 40–41

U

Unauthorized acts................................ 24
Unauthorized practice of
   law... 21–22

V

Venue..40

W

Willingness..8
Wills.. 20

Notes

Notes